AF333081

TEACHING ADULTS IN PUBLIC PLACES

Museums, Parks, Consumer Education Sites

The Professional Practices in Adult Education and Lifelong Learning Series explores issues and concerns of practitioners who work in the broad range of settings in adult and continuing education and lifelong learning.

The books provide information and strategies on how to make practice more effective for professionals and those they serve. They are written from a practical viewpoint and provide a forum for instructors, administrators, policy makers, counselors, trainers, instructional designers, and other related professionals. The series contains single author or coauthored books only and does not include edited volumes.

Sharan B. Merriam
Ronald M. Cervero
Series Editors

TEACHING ADULTS IN PUBLIC PLACES

Museums, Parks, Consumer Education Sites

Edward W. Taylor

KRIEGER PUBLISHING COMPANY
MALABAR, FLORIDA
2012

Original Edition 2012

Printed and Published by
KRIEGER PUBLISHING COMPANY
KRIEGER DRIVE
MALABAR, FLORIDA 32950

FROM A DECLARATION OF PRINCIPLES JOINTLY ADOPTED BY A COMMITTEE OF THE AMERICAN BAR ASSOCIATION AND A COMMITTEE OF PUBLISHERS:

This publication is designed to provide accurate and authoritative information in regard to the subject matter covered. It is sold with the understanding that the publisher is not engaged in rendering legal, accounting, or other professional service. If legal advice or other expert assistance is required, the services of a competent professional person should be sought.

Library of Congress Cataloging-in-Publication Data

Nonformal education : teaching adults in public places / Edward W. Taylor.
   p. cm. — (Professional practices in adult education and lifelong learning series)
 Includes bibliographical references and index.
 ISBN-13: 978-1-57524-291-0 (alk. paper)
 ISBN-10: 1-57524-291-5 (alk. paper)
 1. Adult education. 2. Non-formal education. I. Taylor, Edward W. (Edward Woodbury), 1952-
 LC5219.N66 2011
 374—dc22
                                        2010049167

10 9 8 7 6 5 4 3 2

CONTENTS

PREFACE

This book is an effort to address some of the concerns and misunderstandings about nonformal education and, in particular, nonformal education in developed countries taught in more public places (museums, parks, consumer sites). Here are the specific objectives:

1. To discuss the literature that informs the practice of teaching in nonformal settings.
2. To explore in depth the settings of nonformal education and how this context shapes the educator's practice and the educational experience of the nonformal learner.
3. To discuss researched practices and successful teaching strategies for improving learning that can be applied across a wide variety of nonformal educational situations.
4. To offer a reflective approach to evaluating teaching in nonformal settings.
5. To propose a model of nonformal education for teaching in more public places that considers the complexity of nonformal educational experiences.

Chapter 1 introduces the concept of nonformal education in developed countries through a description a self-help clinic on changing a faucet at a home improvement store. This chapter sets the context for the rest of the book by identifying the central questions to be explored.

Chapter 2 discusses what is presently known about the practice of nonformal education. The objectives include synthesizing the various interpretations of nonformal education, by describing its key characteristics and by analyzing the different conceptual models of nonformal education (Livingstone, 2006; Norland, 2005; Reed & Loughran, 1984; Rogers, 2004, 2005). This chapter will provide an in-depth understanding of the major issues facing nonformal education in developed countries. In addition, Chapter 2 looks at the literature from cultural institutions that describes museum education, environmental education, and consumer education among others that offer insight into the underlying assumptions of teaching and learning in nonformal settings.

Chapters 3, 4, and 5 focus specifically on the practice of teaching in nonformal settings. This information is based on a series of in-depth case studies from consumer education sites, museums, and parks, involving over 40 interviews and lengthy observations of nonformal educators teaching. In particular, Chapter 3 focuses on the unique nonformal context and how it shapes practice. It tries to identify some of the most significant factors such as limited time, volunteerism, and the diversity of learners found in more public places. The goal is to better understand how the nonformal educator can make use of this information in practice.

Chapter 4 focuses on the varied instructional approaches observed and discussed by educators when teaching in nonformal settings. It also discusses how they make sense of practice and it starts to shed light on a shared set of beliefs about teaching that transcend the varied nonformal settings. Despite these new insights, what will be most apparent to the reader is that the nonformal setting is far too complex to assume that there is one instructional approach.

In response to this challenge, Chapter 5 offers a reflexive approach to teaching to assist educators in making their way when teaching in nonformal settings. This involves an ongoing review and self-evaluation of the teaching experience, the educators' role, their relationship to the learners, the teaching setting, and the institutional expectations. The goal is to help the educator become more informed about ways to teach that are responsive to the needs and interests of the nonformal learner.

Chapter 6 offers a new way to look at nonformal education. In particular, it builds on previous models of nonformal education discussed in Chapter 2 (e.g., Brennan, 1997; Rogers, 2005). The chapter provides a new perspective on how to define nonformal education in relationship to formal education. It identifies a type of nonformal education that has been historically overlooked in the nonformal education literature (e.g., cultural institutions). This new framework offers a tool for scholars in organizing future research and provides guidance to the nonformal educator in making sense of teaching in nonformal settings. The final chapter is also reflexive in nature, looking back at this investigative experience. It discusses how the clarification of nonformal education offers direction on where the study of nonformal education should be headed in the future.

ACKNOWLEDGMENTS

I would like to thank all the dedicated nonformal educators who allowed me to observe them teaching and participated in an interview. Their insightful thoughts and personal experiences about teaching helped bring this book to fruition.

CHAPTER 1

Introduction

Recently I was working on changing a faucet in the bathroom on the first floor of my townhouse in Pennsylvania. I began by making a mental note of everything I thought I needed and off I went to the local home improvement retail store. It didn't seem like a difficult project, and I quickly buzzed around the store picking out all the necessary items. Well, like most home improvement projects that are perceived as simple and easy, it didn't turn out that way. I found myself returning to the store several times, picking up items I forgot, returning items that were the wrong size, and seeking out assistance from employees in the plumbing section. Eventually, after several hours if not more, I finally completed my task. However, on one of my trips to the store I noticed that it offered several self-help clinics on a variety of home improvement tasks. The schedule listed tile laying, closet organizing, and basic plumbing.

Fortuitously, there was a clinic offered in the near future on how to change a faucet, and I made a particular point to be there. After attending the clinic I was amazed at how simple it was to change a faucet. Also, with the proper know-how and tools, it could be completed in a much shorter period of time than I had already invested. More interesting were the unique teaching and learning that took place during this clinic. Here was an educational event, nonformal at best, that reflected a number of unique educational challenges rarely seen in formal educational settings or discussed in educational texts. The clinic was handled masterfully by a professional plumber, who had no training, he said, formal or otherwise, in the teaching of adults. Let me begin by describing what I observed.

The instructional clinic was set up in the middle of the plumbing section of a local home improvement store, where there was much foot traffic. Many people, some more interested than others, were walking by a table that was laid out with a variety of equipment and materials used to change a faucet. For demonstration purposes there were a couple of different sinks and several types of faucets, along with relevant tools. As the clinic began, 7 to 10 interested participants began to huddle around one side of the table, with the plumber educator on the other. He started the session without a script, even though I found out later that the home improvement store does provide one and expects it to be followed. He introduced himself and asked the audience what brought them here today and what particular challenges they were having or had had with changing a faucet. He listened attentively to their responses. Mostly the participants were just curious about how to change a faucet if the problem ever arose. Some had questions, such as: "How do you know if you have the right size washer?" and "What should I do first when changing the faucet?" Then he addressed their questions and concerns by answering them directly or mentioning that a particular question would be covered in the clinic. Next he went over all the different items on the table, identifying the tools and types of faucets. He then demonstrated the step-by-step process for changing a faucet, using an actual sink located on the table in front of him. I listened and observed attentively, and soon realized that my experience of changing the faucet would have been made easier by using a tool called a basin wrench. This tool allows you to remove the mounting nuts underneath the sink, without the frustration and difficulty (and sometime smashed knuckles) often found when using a standard wrench.

However, what was more interesting was what was unfolding pedagogically. As a professional educator, I was impressed with the array of challenges that are rarely experienced in the formal setting or discussed in a methods course on teaching adults, and with how easily the plumber educator handled them. For example, the teaching setting or context was chaotic at best. The store announcement system blared out on a regular basis and at times drowned out the presentation. Furthermore, since the session was located near a major thoroughfare, patrons were constantly walking by the clinic. At times, a few customers on the periphery would stop and lean in for a moment, listen to what was being said, and then move on. Others would stay and move in closer, while some of the original participants would drift away. The plumber educator seemed to be aware of the fluidity of learner participation in the clinic. He made a particular point to engage the group through eye contact and humor and by offering a stimulating presentation, hoping to discourage the participants from losing interest, dropping out, and walking away. I observed participants who joined the clinic midway and asked questions that had already been asked by the original participants. Also, along with this ever-shifting group of learners, there wasn't any way for the plumber educator to determine without some lengthy discussion the varying abilities of the learners, what they already knew about plumbing, and if the clinic was addressing their needs. Determining if the clinic was meeting of the needs of the participants seemed to be the responsibility of the learners.

The plumber's response to this chaos was generally unflappable calm. He easily responded to questions that had been previously asked or were new, and then moved back to where he left off, continuing the sequential demonstration of changing a faucet. I did not observe the plumber relying on a text to guide or assist himself through the process. Instead, the content of the clinic as well his responses to questions seemed rooted in his extensive personal experience with plumbing. This was affirmed by comments such as "from my experience" or "I have had much better success by using this tool." Furthermore, he made a particular point to demonstrate each major step of changing a faucet with a good deal of emphasis on a "visual demonstration." Apart from the visual presentation was an opportunity for the participants to touch and pick up any item located on the table. Tools were passed out into the group of learners for them to handle. Interestingly, there didn't seem to be any pedagogical plan. It was as if the task of changing a faucet itself was the plan, whereby the participants were all apprentices observing the necessary steps and strategies of completing a basic task of plumbing.

This educational experience at the home improvement store caused me to reflect on what I had read about nonformal education. A few things of what I remember from the literature seemed consistent with what I had observed in this clinic, such as nonformal education is described as being more responsive to local needs. However, many more things were happening that were not consistent with or had not been discussed or written about in any literature I have read concerning nonformal education. For example, there was a clear hierarchical relationship between the educator and the participants. The plumber educator was the expert and he was dispensing knowledge, sharing information with the participants. The roles of the participants and plumber educator seemed quite defined, which is inconsistent with most of the literature that describes nonformal education as collaborative and learner-centered. In addition, absent from the literature is the array of challenges present in the nonformal environment, such as the distractions associated with teaching in a public setting, the power of volunteerism and its influence on teaching, and the importance of creating a fun and interesting educational experience, just to mention a few.

After this experience, I was awash with questions about nonformal education that I wanted to explore. For example, was this clinic or instructional activity unique when compared with other nonformal educational experiences? Why was there so much happening during this clinic pedagogically that wasn't discussed in the literature on nonformal education? Did the plumber educator see himself as a nonformal educator and if so, how would he describe his role? What role did the store setting have in shaping the nonformal educational experience? Also, how did the learners make meaning of this experience?

WHAT IS NONFORMAL EDUCATION?

Nonformal education is often defined as "any organized, intentional and explicit effort to promote learning to enhance the quality of life through non-school settings" (Heimlich, 1993, p. 2). Although definitions vary greatly, the primary purpose of nonformal education has traditionally been seen as addressing educational concerns that are not adequately covered within formal educational systems. It is seen as providing an alternative educational medium for populations that have been overlooked or underserved by formal systems, most often associated with international development programs. In developed countries nonformal education is often located in more public settings and has received little attention within the field, particularly within North America.

Nonformal education in more public places, wherein access by the general population is greater and easier, is everywhere and most likely a more prevalent form of education than what takes place in formal settings across the country. For example, let's go back to the home improvement clinic. At the time I wrote this chapter there were over 3000 Home Depot and Lowe's home improvement stores in the United States, making them the two largest home improvement retailers in the country. Most of them offer several clinics on the weekends and evenings at their stores. Based on my observations, the levels of participation ranged between 3 to 15 learners per session. It would be safe to assume that on any given weekend 15,000 people are attending clinics in the United States and Canada, a number equivalent to enrollment at a mid-sized university or community college. This number is immense when considering that it is only one type of nonformal education in a more public setting. Also, this number doesn't begin to include the smaller home improvement stores across the country that offer similar clinics.

When we start to broaden the scope to include nonformal education in cultural institutions, where public access is generally available, millions of adults can be found gathering every day in libraries, parks, zoos, aquariums, and museums across North America. For example, each year more than 287 million people visit the 391 units of parks, monuments, national recreation areas, battlefields, wild and scenic rivers, and seashores of the national parks in the United States (National Park Service, 2007). During these visits, many adults often meet a park interpreter and participate in local nonformal education programs, such as a trail tour of park vegetation and wildlife, a discussion on land management practices, or a hands-on exploration of the geology in the park.

The circle of nonformal education participation continues to grow even further when you consider, for example, nonformal education for adults in libraries. For instance, the staff of the Dauphin County Library in Harrisburg, Pennsylvania, organizes a monthly book discussion called "Novel Thoughts Book Club" (Dauphin County Library System, 2009). The same is true for zoos and museums. In the San Diego Zoo, individuals can be found participating in a "Roar & Snore Adults Only Night" involving a walk at dusk through the Heart of Africa and the Lion Camp (San Diego Zoo,

2009). Across the United States people can be found gathering for a tour of slave quarters located on Carter's Grove in Williamsburg, Virginia, learning about the rich complexity of the African American culture and the slaves' meager existence during this historic period (Colonial Williamsburg, 2008).

At this point, even though participation of adults most likely far surpasses what goes on in formal settings, it is mind-boggling to begin to try to make sense of the level of participation, the range of content, and the various teaching approaches that are engaged in on any given weekend or evening in a nonformal setting.

One would think with all this nonformal education energy going on locally in this country that there would be a good deal of interest about teaching in these more public settings. However, despite its ubiquitous presence, there has been little empirical attention given to nonformal education in more public places within the field of adult education. What research exists is found predominantly within specific disciplines, such as museum education, consumer education, environmental education, and historical interpretation to mention a few. There has been little appreciation of similar contextual challenges and teaching approaches that transcend the various settings. Furthermore, most of this research focuses predominantly on program evaluation and learner/audience outcomes (e.g., Beckman, 1999; Brody & Tomkiewicz, 2002; Hitch & Youatt, 2002; Manikowske, Stone, Farr, Wilson, & Wintersteen, 2002; Pedretti, Macdonald, Gitari, & McLaughlin, 2001; Verdurme & Viaene, 2003). This literature gives little attention to the nature of nonformal education and how the nonformal educator makes sense of practice. What was cited by Reed back in 1984 is still consistent today:

> Practitioners assume that NFE makes a diverse, useful, and more pervasive influence on most individuals, and on community development, than does formal education. Documentation of this assumption is meager, but given the wide range of agencies and organizations that deliver NFE compared with schooling, it is safe to claim that the quantity of learning is much larger and more diverse. (pp. 52-53)

There are several explanations for the lack of attention to nonformal education. Most significant is whether nonformal education as a category is contributing to an understanding of adult education in developed countries (Merriam & Caffarella, 1999). Even though the description is somewhat accurate for developing countries, in developed countries it is argued that many nonformal learning opportunities seem more similar to programs found in formal educational institutions. Despite this concern, Merriam and Caffarella see the category as having import:

> . . . both in terms of recognizing the many educational programs in developing countries as well as focusing on the community–based programs of adult learning in all environments that fit the parameters of less structure, more flexibility, and concern for social inequalities. (p. 29)

Similarly, Brennan (1997), who has analyzed nonformal education in developing countries, makes a strong argument for its significance and cultural specificity. The recognition and exploration of nonformal education not only help address its historical neglect, as the poor cousin of the formal system, but offer much for formal education, which can "adapt strategies and processes that have been shown to be successful in the NFE system" (p. 198). Even though his analysis offers little insight into the everyday practice of nonformal education in more public places and cultural institutions and is generally limited to developing countries, his reconceptualization offers a framework that helps make sense of different types of nonformal education. Brennan's framework is discussed in more depth in Chapter 2.

Even as nonformal education is debated for its applicability in developed countries, the lack of clarity in the definition of nonformal education has also contributed to its disuse. Bock and Papagiannis (1983) shed light on this problem:

> Nonformal education as an educational term is loaded with different shades of meaning, and these meanings vary according to the context—revolutionary, non-revolutionary, under-

developed, developing—and according to one's philosophical views of the role of education in general. (p. 14)

Characteristically, nonformal education is often described in the literature as more present-time focused, responsive to localized needs, learner-centered, less structured, and with an assumed nonhierarchical relationship between the learner and facilitator (Bock & Bock, 1989; Coombs & Ahmed, 1974; Courtenay, 1991; Ewert, 1989; Jarvis, 1987; Marsick & Watkins, 1990; Merriam & Caffarella, 1999; Reed & Loughran, 1984). In addition, though little is written about it, nonformal education experiences pose a variety of teaching challenges often not found to such a degree in formal educational settings. For example, learners can come and go at their choosing; participation is voluntary; there is often a wide variety of abilities and ages among learners; there are regularly ongoing distractions, particularly in outdoor and public settings; and educational personnel are often hired to teach for their content expertise and may have little systematic teacher training (Taylor, 2006). Unfortunately, what literature is available is generally anecdotally based and often shares similar sources with little critical analysis of its meaning and in-depth understanding of what actually happens in local nonformal settings.

At this point, it may be argued that due to the nature of the term or category that further work is not warranted in this area. In other words, nonformal education as a concept and idea does not adequately capture the educational complexity associated with the breadth of educational settings and practices that are taking place outside the formal system. Possibly, leaving it up to different areas such as museum, consumer, and library education to make meaning of their individual settings will allow for a greater understanding to emerge. However, I would argue that the reverse has happened based on the present evidence. As the research emphasis on nonformal education has shifted to the varying areas, there has been a silo effect, with little sharing between the different disciplines and little cross fertilization, thus creating a myopic view of education outside the formal system. Further, many settings and forms of local nonformal education are not captured within these broad disciplines. Educators have little to turn to when seeking ways to improve practice. Without an effort to make meaning of the whole, the successful practices of the various nonformal programs are inadequately understood and appreciated among the many settings within the large tent of nonformal education.

Furthermore, society today is paying greater attention to lifelong learning. Some adults are choosing leisure activities and projects, others are being pressured to continually learn (e.g., new job skills) throughout their lives, and much of this education is taking place outside the formal system. To understand this trend, the varying teaching contexts, and a means to improve practice, we need a clearer and more meaningful picture of nonformal education.

CONCLUSION

The idea of studying nonformal education began with an everyday experience of observing teaching in a local home improvement retail store. This experience provoked a foray into the relevant literature about nonformal education and became the catalyst for an extensive investigation into a form of education, ubiquitous across the educational landscape, but inadequately appreciated and understood. As readers move on into the rest of the book, they will be surprised by both the complexity of teaching in nonformal settings and the implication this research has for improving practice for both nonformal and formal education.

CHAPTER 2

Defining Nonformal Education

Looking back on the plumbing clinic in the local hardware store, discussed in Chapter 1, it is apparent that there is much happening from an educational perspective. To better understand what is going on when teaching in nonformal settings, two areas of literature can be helpful: first, nonformal education information and second, discipline specific information about teaching located in consumer sites and cultural institutions such as museums, libraries, zoos, and natural settings. An overview of relevant information provides a useful context from which to begin understanding the complexities of teaching in such settings. The chapter begins with an overview of nonformal education, followed by a discussion of relevant literature from teaching and learning in cultural institutions.

DEFINITIONS

Nonformal education is most often referred to by its classical definition of a "motley assortment of organized and semi-organized educational activities operating outside the regular structure and routines of the formal [educational] system, aimed at serving a great variety of learning needs of different subgroups in the population young and old" (Ahmed & Coombs, 1975, p. xxix). Similarly, Reed and Loughran (1984) define it as "any organized, intentional and explicit effort to promote learning to enhance of the quality of life through out-of-school approaches" (p. 52). Kleis (as cited in Harmon, 1976) offers further clarification. Nonformmal education is defined:

Not by the absence, but by the non-centrality, of form, by the persistent subordination of form from mission. A mission or objective, on the one hand, and an educational mechanism designed to achieve objectives, on the other, merge as essential characteristics of nonformal education. (p. 5)

These definitions reveal that typically nonformal education is often defined in relationship to formal education, or the institutionalized school system, and although organized, nonformal education is outside of a formal centralized educational system.

Essentially nonformal education is characterized as opposite to what is seen as typically formal education, as "not formal education" (Norland, 2005, p. 6). By the constant comparison to formal education, the descriptions tend to focus on what it is not, as opposed to better understanding its purpose and what happens in the everyday nonformal education practice. An example of the characteristics used to differentiate nonformal from formal education is provided in Table 2.1. The table draws on three individual models developed previously by Norland (2006. p. 8), Rogers (1992, p. 26), and Torres (2001, p. 6).

Although initially helpful because the binary comparison offers an easy and quick way to make sense of nonformal education, the table oversimplifies the complexity that exists in making meaning of nonformal education. Furthermore, it gives the illusion that there are distinct boundaries between these concepts. In reality there is much overlap. For example, where in the table would a self-help clinic on plumbing be located? It could, based on the table, be considered formal education because of its governance inclusive of paid staff and resources provided by large corporation. Yet, it could also be considered nonformal education, because of its short-term goals (helping consumers with an immediate home fix-up), its complementary orientation (addressing a need not provided by the formal system), flexible structure (offering courses on weekends), open participation, and evaluation via self-assessment.

In addition to the lack of distinction between these categories is the simplicity projected in characteristics to describe teaching in nonformal settings, such as learner-centered, with a low structure program design and flexible curriculum. Thinking about these descriptors in reference to the plumbing clinic at the home improvement store discussed in Chapter 1, it is apparent that several of these characteristics don't apply. Later in the book, recent research will

Table 2.1 Comparison of Nonformal and Formal Education

	Nonformal	Formal
Objective	• Address immediate needs • Foster social change • Personal growth	• Long-term needs • Promote the status quo
Main Agent/Provider Status	• Civil society/NGOs • Public: community ownership • Project: ad-hoc, temporary • Satellite • Complementary	• Government/Ministry education • Public: state ownership • Policy: institutionalized structured permanent • Mainstream
Beneficiaries	• Poorest • Groups with specific needs	• Poor • All members of society
Cost	• Volunteers • Stipend • More cost effective	• Salaried personnel • Remuneration • More costly
Curriculum/Content	• Flexible • Options • Variety	• Sequential • Fixed
Role of the Educator/Learner	• Learnerer-centered	• Teacher-centered
Program Design	• Low structure • Open • Voluntary • On site • Not organized • Continuing	• High structure • Selective • Mandatory • Off site • Rigid • Terminal
Time	• Immediate	• Future
Resources	• Local • Decentralized • Low costs	• State • Federal • Centralized • High cost
Evaluation	• Self-assessing	• Validated by change

show that at times teaching in a nonformal setting is highly structured and teacher-centered. Furthermore, what can't be revealed in this binary framework is the interrelationship between the nonformal setting and the educator, and how they influence and shape the educational experience.

RELATIONSHIP TO OTHER FORMS OF EDUCATION

Nonformal education is not only discussed in relationship to formal education, but also in relationship to other forms of education, which include informal and incidental education. These other categories help further differentiate nonformal education, but at the same time challenge the classification process. Evans (1981) provides a scheme that helps explain these categories in relationship to nonformal and informal education.

- Incidental education. Learning takes place without either a conscious attempt to present on the part of the source or a conscious attempt to learn on the part of the learner.
- Informal education. Learning results from situations where either the learner or the source of information, but not both, has a conscious intent of promoting learning.
- Nonformal education. This is any non-school learning where both the source and the learner have a conscious intent to promote learning.
- Formal education. This differs from nonformal education by its location within institutions called schools, which are characterized by the use of age-graded classes of youth being taught a fixed curriculum by a cadre of certified teachers using standard pedagogical methods. (p. 28)

Incidental and informal learning reflect most of the learning experienced by adults in their lifetime. Incidental learning happens outside the learner's conscious awareness, while informal learning involves a conscious effort on the learner's part, such as learning how to play the guitar or taking a self-guided tour of a museum. However, when the learner and the source (e.g., teacher) both make a conscious effort to promote learning outside a formal setting, then the learner is engaged in nonformal education.

Further challenging the process of clarifying nonformal education is the emergence of other concepts that are at times used synonymously or are often closely associated with nonformal education. These include lifelong, complementary, alternative, recurrent, and continuing education, and free-choice learning. For example, lifelong education is seen as encompassing all forms of learning. It has been defined as:

> A process of accomplishing personal, social and professional development throughout the life-span of individuals. . . . It is a comprehensive and unifying idea, which includes formal, non-formal and informal learning for acquiring and enhancing enlightenment so as to attain the fullest possible development in different stages and domains of life. (Dave, 1976, p. 34)

Another concept is complementary education, which refers to educational experiences designed to complement the formal system, such as literacy programs for adults and adult high schools (Brennan, 1999; Evans, 1981; Silberman-Keller, 2006). Similarly, recurrent education, a concept advocated by the Organization for Economic Cooperation and Development (OECD), is defined as:

> A comprehensive educational strategy for all post-compulsory or post-basic education, the essential characteristic of which is the distribution of education over the total life-span of the individual in a recurring way, i.e., in alternation with other activities, principally with work, but also with leisure and retirement. (OECD, 1973, p. 16)

Recurrent education, like complementary education, has its roots in human capital theory (skills and knowledge that have economic value) and is more utilitarian and associated with the world of work and vocation.

As this discussion unfolds it is important to know that there are few, if any, clear definitions and neat answers available in make meaning of this nonformal education. For example, for many learning events that are classified as nonformal education, an equal argument can be made that they are more like formal, out of school, participatory, and/or community education, just to mention a few. Nonformal education is a term that is constantly evolving. Like any educational endeavors it is greatly influenced by context/setting and by the educator and the learner who are engaged in the event. Other influences are institutional goals and the social, historical forces shaping society at a given time.

ORIGINS

Another way to develop an understanding of nonformal education is to explore its roots. Some would argue that nonformal education has been around as long as humans have been engaged in ways of educating each other (Reed, 1984). However, not until the early 1960s did it become an educational phenomenon that was formally studied (Bock & Papagiannis, 1983; Coombs, 1975, 1968). In Coombs's (1975) view, nonformal education predates formal education by many centuries, although most educators see it as a contemporary concept. He cites:

> Organized human societies from the beginning have used various forms of what we have come to call nonformal education to transmit their heritage of values, customs, beliefs, technologies and skills to each new generation, thus insuring the survival and integrity of these societies, each with its own uniqueness. (p. 282)

Examples would include religious ceremonies and instruction, apprenticeships, and tribal puberty rites.

From a more contemporary perspective, nonformal education was seen as response to the educational needs for learners that were not adequately met by the formal system, in particular the rural poor. Bock and Papagiannis (1983) state:

> Schooling is unable to the meet the educational or learning

needs of the rural poor of the world. Nonformal education, as a substitute for or a complment to schooling, could with proper implementation design and planning, alleviate this educational deprivation and thus contribute to rural transformation. (p. 6)

The literature of nonformal education is a product of three different but related groups. The first group, though less prolific but much more active, includes the actual practitioners of nonformal education who are directly involved in helping the marginalized and impoverished individuals in the world through programs in literacy, consumer education, farmer education, family planning, for example. The second group is the international educational planners who question the capability of the formal education system to make a difference developmentally in the world. These development specialists have seen firsthand the inadequacies of the formal system of education in undeveloped countries. A final group is made up of the critics of the formal system, such as Freire and Illich, who writing from a social justice perspective. They see the formal system as reproducing the status quo, further embedding marginalized people in oppressive structures of society, and nonformal education as a means for liberation and social justice (Evans, 1981). Nonformal education, even though it always is working under the large shadow of the formal system, is seen as possessing definitive characteristics that give it a greater advantage to respond to the educational needs of marginalized groups than the dominant system. These advantages include its propensity for immediate action, its learning opportunities for direct application, and its close proximity and accessibility for those in need of education (Brembeck, 1973).

There was much hope and potential seen in nonformal education addressing the shortcomings of formal education in the 1960s. Formal education was struggling to meet the demands of a growing student population, increasing educational costs, lack of resources, poorly trained staff, and overall inadequate infrastructure. A response to these shortcomings of the formal system resulted in what Coombs and others call the promotion of "rapid expansion of nonformal education" particularly within developing countries (Bock & Papagiannis, 1976, p. 7). Advocates of this position believe nonformal education acted as a powerful intervention for promoting international development. More specifically, it was seen as a means to accomplish the following:

1. Provide education to those for whom schooling is not a realistic alternative.
2. Make new skills and attitudes available to the rural poor.
3. Circumvent cultural obstacles that prevent some peoples from utilizing school effectively.
4. Use scarce educational resources more efficiently.
5. Modify the educational system itself. (Deleon cited in Bock & Papagiannis, 1976, p. 8)

Overall nonformal education was seen as a way to reach and impact the lives of more people and by less expensive means. Underlying assumptions that frame this perspective of nonformal education include the belief that change in the social structure comes from the education of marginalized individuals.

Although beyond the scope of this book, there are alternative perspectives that found this model of development too rooted in an overly psychological Western view of personal enlightenment, without taking into account the social structure and context of the educational endeavor, and in particular, failing to recognize the " 'centrality of power' in relationship between education and other social systems" (Bock & Papagiannis, 1976, p. 9). By attempting to foster social change through a human capital deficit model of education, actually, development was impeded by further reenforcing social hierarchies through the easing of social pressure on power structures (placating the disenfranchised) and further embedding the rural poor in everyday oppression (Bock & Papagiannis, 1976; Taylor, 1994). Seen as a corrective education intervention, nonformal education, like education in general, can be viewed in its own right as a system of socialization shaped and influenced by society. All this being said reminds the reader of a fundamental premise of what this book is founded—upon that for nonformal education, like any education, formal or otherwise, to be truly understood, "it must be studied within the societal context in which it occurs, as its terms and its content"(Bock & Papagiannis, 1976, p. 17).

CONTEMPORARY PERSPECTIVES

Recently, nonformal education as a concept and as a practice has been going through a renewal, although the uncertainty and lack of clarity associated with the concept continue. Nonformal education has been seen in the discourse of a growing number of fields, such as environmental education, distance education, and other sciences. Further, with this expansion the boundaries are continually blurred where and how nonformal education is associated with educational interventions across age groups and within and outside formal settings. Rogers (2005) concludes that:

> This newer discourse with its sense of a unified education stretching throughout the whole of life (both lifelong and life wide) has created the need for some kinds of distinction within this unity, and this has led to a revived use of the terminology of NFE. (p. 235)

Nonformal education, born out of the insufficiencies of the formal education system, is often seen in contrast to, as a binary, something that was better than, and complementary to formal education. Nonformal education is the place for innovation and creative educational strategies and all the while formal education was seen as resistant to change, homogenous, and rigid (Torres, 2001). Torres further stipulates:

> Many of the characteristics typically attributed to NFE, when contrasted with FE—such as flexibility, school-community linkages, openness and responsiveness to the needs and possibilities of the learners and to specific contexts and cultures, etc.—are characteristics that describe *good* education, regardless of the specific modality it adopts and regardless of the age, gender, social, economic, ethnic and cultural conditions of learners. (p. 5)

In response to the uncritical use of the term of nonformal education, the growing interest toward a unified educational experience as lifelong, and the emergence of diverse educational programs and systems worldwide that resist classification have prompted the need for a reconceptualization of nonformal education (Rogers, 2004, 2005; Torres, 2001). To understand the various ways nonformal education has evolved, two recent efforts are discussed below.

An Integrated Perspective

A recent re-conceptualization sees nonformal education as "an integrated force which has the potential to serve developing nations to a degree perhaps equal to, if not greater, than formal education that has attracted most of the attention and the resources in developing nations" (Brennan, 1997, p. 198). He identifies three conceptual tools (system, setting, and process) to help shed light on the nature of nonformal education in itself, rather than in relationship to formal education.

As an educational *system,* nonformal education is often decentralized and unstructured, such that it can vary in character from community to community with no central or bureaucratic office to manage its affairs. As a *setting,* nonformal education is found most often outside the formal system, both as an educational endeavor that is unsupervised by the formal system and as one that is generally located at the site of the educational need. As a *process,* he argues that certain "teaching and learning strategies of nonformal education need to be appropriate to the learners, their culture and the objectives of the programmes concerned" (p. 190). In other words, teaching nonformal education may vary from the formal system.

Using these conceptual tools, Brennan identifies three types of nonformal education. The first type is seen as a *complement* to the formal system by addressing needs that are not adequately met by the formal system (e.g., school dropouts, adult literacy). A second type is seen as an *alternative* to the formal system that seeks to recognize indigenous education. "Indigenous education and learner refer to structures and practices that existed before colonization and continued to exist in some form for some features of personal and community life after colonization" (p. 187). The third type of nonformal education is seen as a *supplement* to the formal system, one which is designed to address needs of developing nations. For example, the educational needs following the collapse of the Communist world included gaining an understanding of capitalism and the related economic and political issues. Brennan states:

> This type of NFE is required as a quick reaction to educational, social and economic needs because the formal education is too slow in its response (if it does in fact decide to respond) to these needs. (p. 187)

In response to this framework, questions are raised about how this informs nonformal education in developing countries? Where do zoos, libraries, museums, and natural parks fit into this framework? For example, in relationship to Brennan's three types of nonformal education (complement, alternative, supplement), education in parks, museums, and consumer sites could be found in each of these types. Clearly, museum education complements what is learned in formal settings and many schools and universities use museums to do just that. Furthermore, these sites also offer an alternative approach to the formal system, and at times are designed in such a way to address the needs of marginalized groups. For example, a UNESCO initiative, where museums were seen as having potential for fostering development among disenfranchised, is the Pinacoteca do Estado de São Paulo art museum that "set up the Social-Cultural Inclusion Programme, which aims to increase accessibility for certain groups that suffer exclusion, such as sex workers, the homeless and young children in risk situations" (Cabral, 2005, p. 12). And, these institutions can also be seen as supplementing the larger society by offering venues that engage the public in discussion about core societal values (e.g., peace, war, sustainability, capitalism). For example, supplementing cultural institutions include the Holocaust Museum, Everglades National Park, and the future Canadian Museum for Human Rights, just to mention a few.

Despite these shortcomings, this framework (system, setting, process) offers some understanding of how these institutions play an educational role in the larger society and is part and parcel of

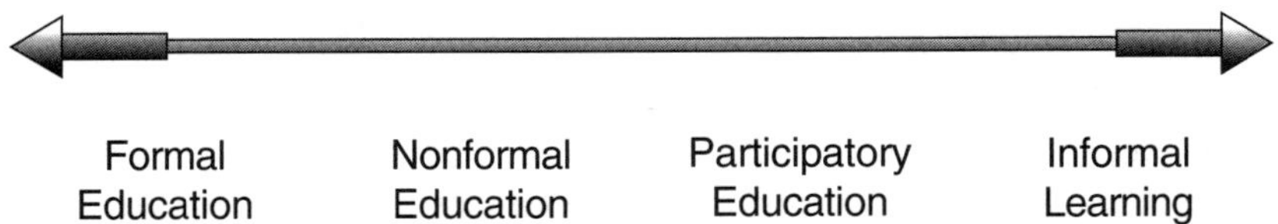

Figure 2.1 The continuum of education (Rogers, 2004).

nonformal education. However, when the discussion moves to the level of practice, it falls well short of capturing what is unique about teaching in the nonformal settings.

A Continuum Perspective

The focus of a continuum perspective of nonformal education is more about its relationship to other forms of education. Rogers (2004, 2005) says that discussing nonformal education as a concept and practice is important because it reminds educators that there are other educational means and opportunities outside the formal system, with the potential to promote activism and educational reform. He offers a new perspective of nonformal education, where it is placed not in opposition to other categories of education, but on a continuum located in relationship to other categories. This allows for educational programs (e.g., museums, literacy groups, public schools) to be placed anywhere on the continuum based on the degree they reflect the characteristics of a particular category. Figure 2.1 shows four key concepts that make up the continuum of education: formal education, nonformal education, participatory education, and informal learning.

To better understand how the different concepts relate to each other it is necessary to discuss three related characteristics, those of flexibility, participation, and contextualization. Rogers (2005) sees flexibility at the heart of nonformal education. It is for example:

> The ability to employ nonprofessional or paraprofessional teachers; the need to adapt the curriculum or to develop new curricula to meet local needs; and it is . . . the need to develop locally determined timetables rather than a national uniform programme. (p. 249)

Much of nonformal education, particularly in developing countries, reflects what Rogers refers to as nonformal schooling, "alternative and more flexible forms of schooling" (p. 250). In relationship to the continuum in Figure 2.1, an educational program that is more flexible and responsive to local or individual needs moves to the right. A program moves in the opposite direction if it reflects a more standardized program, which is less responsive to individual needs, such as a chemistry course at a community college. The concept of flexibility is related to another key characteristic, that of participation, or the degree of involvement by learners in their educational endeavors.

Participation is assessed in several areas of an educational experience as the degree to which the following occurs:

- Learners attend an educational event and take up the information and apply it to their lives.
- Learners actively engage in the educational activities within the course/class rather than as passive recipients.
- Learners take responsibility and share in some of the decision making of the educational experience.

It is this last degree of participation that brings further clarity to the various categories. For example, Rogers (2005) sees nonformal education, within a development context, as having limited participation, not as a fully participatory form of education. Nonformal education is referred to as flexible schooling, because the provider often determines local control, and the learner has a limited range of decision making (limited participation). On the other hand, participatory education is distinguished from nonformal education based on the degree of participation. Participatory education is found in programs where learners "determine the contents and time scale of the learning program as well as the logistics" (p. 255). As with flexibility, learners experience greater participation as educational programs move to the right on the continuum. The extreme would be informal learning, where individuals direct their own learning. And, on the other end, generally in formal settings, participation in decision making by learners is minimal, having little impact on the formal educational experience.

The third characteristic, using the language of organizational theory and group dynamics, is the degree to which context, the local setting, shapes the educational program. The more contextualized a program, the more it is personalized to local and individual needs and interests. The less contextualized, the greater degree of standardization, such as in formal groups. For example, the curriculum in a college science course is the same regardless of who participates. As an educational program becomes more flexible and participatory (moving to the right on the continuum), it is more responsive to the specific context and becomes less standardized and more receptive to engaging local interest and needs.

Furthermore, it is important to note that Rogers (2004) does not see these differing conceptualizations of education as categories, because the boundaries between them are gray and not fixed, although the distinctions are real, particularly in relationship to previously discussed characteristics. He concludes:

> Learning is the keystone; it is the original matter out of which all education is created. Somewhere along the learning continuum, we come to purposeful and assisted learning (education in its widest sense). When we control this and individualise it, learn what we want for as long as we want and stop when we want, we are engaging in informal education. When we step into a pre-existing learning programme but mould it to our own circumstances, we are engaged in non-formal education. When we surrender our autonomy and join a programme and accept its externally imposed discipline, we are immersed in formal education. (p. 20)

The strength in Rogers's framework is that it begins to shed light on the relationship between key constructs (flexibility, participation, and contextualization), and how they give meaning to nonformal education. As an educational event becomes less standardized, the more flexible, participatory, and responsive it is to local needs and interest. However, in Rogers's description the relationship only runs along a linear continuum, that is, less standardization means greater flexibility and participation and vice versa. This overlooks the complexity of everyday teaching in a nonformal setting, particularly the wherewithal by the nonformal educator to shape practice. For example, it was observed that consumer educators in home improvement retail stores overlooked a highly standardized scripted curriculum provided by the national office. And, at the same time, their approach to teaching was very structured, but generally not planned, and the degree of visitor participation was limited regardless of clinics observed.

Looking back, it is apparent that the nonformal education literature provides some insight into teaching in this unique educational setting. In particular, there is the recognition that nonformal education exists and is an educational medium to be reckoned with, that it has something to contribute to practice in more formal settings, and also has its own unique challenges. However, there is still an overreliance on arbitrary, anecdotal, and untested assumptions (e.g., flexible, learner-centered) and a failure to recognize the everyday realities of teaching in nonformal settings. Furthermore, much of the interest of nonformal education is rooted in social activism, with interest in addressing the needs of marginalized groups often quite distant (mentally and physically) from the general public. This narrow emphasis overlooks the ever-present teaching that takes place in cultural institutions that do not operate with this agenda.

NONFORMAL EDUCATION IN CULTURAL INSTITUTIONS

In response to a lack of understanding about teaching in nonformal settings, and since the research for this book has been from museums, parks, and consumer education sites, it only seems appropriate to look at how the literature from these cultural institutions helps inform the understanding of teaching in nonformal settings. Like nonformal education there has not been much research on teaching in these cultural institutions either, mostly due to the idea that these sites are generally thought of as places where learners predominantly explore on their own or with others without guidance of a teacher or a guide. As a result, most research has focused on the visitors, for better understanding the reasons that draw them to museums or libraries; how learning is facilitated through exhibits; what keeps visitors engaged while on-site, and what are the learning outcomes of visitor visits. Even though, in general, visitors engage many of these sites without assistance, almost all cultural institution sites are also sites of nonformal education. Teachers, guides, docents, and volunteers provide information as the need arises and may provide more structured tours. In fact, in many cases, without a guide, some museums and parks would be inaccessible to the local public, both intellectually and physically.

Institutions such as museums and natural parks are similar in many ways: social and historical development, educational philosophy and objectives, epistemological tensions, and challenges associated when attracting and educating adult visitors. Therefore it makes sense to discuss what they offer to the understanding of nonformal education as a group than to discuss each separately (Taylor, Parrish, Banz, 2010). This premise is based on the idea that these nonformal sites fall within a shared frame. "They are similarly founded and driven, and . . . inspire similar cognitive acts. Perhaps they are treasuries of a culture, but they are not passive" (Carr, 1991, p. 81). They are also sites of contested and dynamic repositories of knowledge where the education of adults is inherent to their mission (Borg, Cauchi, & Mayo, 2006; Chadwick & Stannett, 2000). As places of adult learning and teaching, these institutions offer a perspective of nonformal education that has been historically overlooked and poorly understood within the field of adult education (Bekerman, Burbules, & Silberman-Keller, 2006; Dudzinska-Przesmitzki & Grenier, 2008; Taylor, 2006).

To better understand these institutions, how they inform the study of nonformal education and more specifically teaching, it is helpful to discuss them in relationship to more formal institutions. This comparison rests on the idea that museums, libraries, and parks "make different assumptions about learners" and the "invitation to learn and conditions for knowing are different" (Carr, 1991, p. 219) than what is generally found in more formal settings. Here is a list of characteristics about nonformal education in cultural institutions, recognizing that the opposite would be descriptive of more formal institutions. Cultural institutions:

- Emphasize informal independent learners, controlled by their own decision and authority over time and attention. . . .

- Communicate through direct multi-sensate experiences with objects and persons; sensual, nonverbal is essential. . . .
- Present information in alinear and discontinuous patterns; the learner can organize them independently. . . .
- Employ both explicit or mandated curricula; . . . individual study is the norm;
- Do not evaluate the learner; do not challenge the learner to perform; do not award credentials or certificates;
- Organize themselves by criteria other than audience age, grade, or gender; access to knowledge and experience is typically not restricted;
- Offer intentionally intergenerational experiences;
- Refer by evidence and inference to worlds and communities outside themselves. (p. 219)

This list of characteristics is similar to some extent to the characteristics discussed earlier in this chapter. Likewise, it somewhat oversimplifies the relationship between public cultural institutions and more formal settings. Furthermore, it both complements and highlights characteristics often not considered when making sense of nonformal education, such as for example, the emphasis on inter-generational experiences found in these educational locations and the open access to knowledge often associated with these sites. Despite this new perspective, little direction, unfortunately, is provided about how these site-specific characteristics inform the practice of teaching. In response to this concern, there are several constructs (interpretive communities, sites of free choice, and public spaces of learning) discussed within these cognate areas that offer insight to the practice of nonformal education in public places.

Interpretation

Interpretation is a concept that explains what visitors and educators do as they spend time in museums, zoos, libraries, and other cultural institutions. From the visitors' perspective, interpretation reveals the process of meaning-making as individuals encounter objects in response to an inherent need for understanding. Rooted in hermeneutics, interpretation explains a relationship (verbal, tacitly, and somatically) between the visitor or learner and the object. It is "where meaning is modified as further relationships are encountered. The encounter between an individual subject and the object is influenced by prior experience and knowledge" (Hooper-Greenfield, 2000, p. 117). In essence, interpretation explains how both the educator and the visitor make meaning of an object that has some value or interest to them. It recognizes that individuals are always seeking meaning and patterns in the world, regardless of setting, connecting their experience to what they determine as significant. This complex and active process reminds the nonformal educator that there is no "knowledge outside the knower—that knowledge is brought into being by the meaning each individual makes of the experiences that she/he has" (p. 118).

Interpretation also has significant implications for the nonformal educator as way of informing practice, or in this case as an interpreter. As a form of practice, it is referred to by Tilden (2007) as a form of provocation with the intent to reveal the larger truth behind any statement or fact. The interpreter's role in a majestic natural park, for example, is to stimulate visitors' thinking so they reflect and thoughtfully recognize the significance of the beauty before them, instead of haphazardly and/or unknowingly overlooking the significance of what stands before them. He defines interpretation as "an educational activity, which aims to reveal meanings and relationships through the use of original objects, by first-hand experience, and by illustrative media, rather than simply to communicate factual information" (Tilden, 2007, p. 33).

What makes for a successful interpretation is always under discussion. For example, authors have argued that interpretation principles should include accuracy, enjoyment, and involvement. They should be holistic, organized, passionate, provocative, relevant, and thematic, just to mention a few characteristics (Davidson & Black, 2007). A recent participatory study of successful guided cave interpretation identified nine principles. Most of them transcend this particular setting and have implications for teaching in a variety of nonformal sites. These principles include:

1.   Visitor enjoyment: Interpretation activities should be designed for visitor enjoyment; this principle is sometimes called entertainment.

2. Relevance to the audience and site: Interpretation needs to be both relevant to the audience and the actual feature being interpreted.
3. Organized: Interpretation must be well-organized so visitors can easily follow what is presented.
4. Key theme: Interpretation should have a key theme/message that has the capacity to tie all the key pieces of information together.
5. Group management: The guide strives to make each person feel recognized as an individual but also as belonging to the group.
6. Protection: The guide provides an experience in which participants feel safe and in which the environment itself is safe.
7. Two-way communication: The interpretive exchange works best if two-way communication is used. At times the guide is an active listener and the group participates in sending messages.
8. Holistic approach: The guide provides an interpretation of the site that demonstrates the site's relationship beyond the immediate area (this may be ecologically, socially, or other).
9. Emotion: The guide is facilitating an experience that gives emotional dimensions to place and people. (p. 32)

Reviewing these guidelines will continue to broaden the understanding of the unique challenges (e.g., engaging emotions, promoting enjoyment) and practices that arise when teaching in nonformal settings.

Free Choice

A more contemporary term that focuses on learning outside the formal system is free choice learning, a concept that helps explain education both outside compulsory settings and as a lifelong endeavor (Falk, 2004). It encompasses both nonformal education and informal learning. Free choice learning is "the most common type of learning in which people engage. It is self-directed, voluntary, guided by individual needs and interests—learning that we engage in throughout our lives" (Falk & Dierking, 2002, p. 9). This concept rests on the ability of the learner to choose, to make a choice of not only what to learn, but with whom and where. It includes learning in organized settings with an instructor and learning that is entirely self-directed. It is argued that free choice learning more accurately captures the learning that takes place in museums, parks, and zoos, than what is described under informal or nonformal education. It is seen as a concept that "recognizes the unique characteristics of such learning—free choice, non-sequential, self-paced, and voluntary" (Falk, 2004, p. 272). It is learning that is internally motivated and driven, rooted in positive attributes, and is seen as knowledge driven, where the individual is perceived to be in control of the learning.

Three main sectors of society provide opportunities for learning: the workplace, universities and public schools, and free choice learning. The free choice sector is less concerned about the site or location of learning. Instead, the emphasis is on choice and the why, what, and how people learn in the everyday life outside formal systems. It includes, for example, learning how to change a tire, searching for information on the internet on how to cook barbecued chicken, or attending a class on stained-glass design. It is a byproduct of developed countries where there is discretionary income and leisure time is more plentiful.

In many nonformal institutions, such as museums, parks, and libraries, free choice brings to light the factors that are most influential in shaping the visitor's learning experience. One factor is how successful visitors are at navigating within the actual space where the material is located, such as exhibits or stacks of books. A visitor's confidence in becoming oriented to these complex environments has significant influence on learning. For nonformal institutions, this means recognizing the importance of how the context attracts and encourages visitors in fully engaging the learning environment. Advanced organizers and design issues, such as color, lightning, sound, and space, have a significant impact on assisting the learner (Falk, 2004).

Another factor, previously discussed, is developing an understanding of the visitors' prior knowledge and motivations for participating in free choice settings. It is assumed that the more the nonformal educator understands visitor expectations and, at the same time, gives them more control over the learning experience, the more these actions can significantly influence learning. "It also means that one should expect learning to be highly personal and strongly influenced by an individual's past knowledge, previous museum experiences, and personal interests" (Falk, 2004, p. 285)

Commons

Important to understanding nonformal education includes not only making sense of the role of the visitor and educator, but also understanding the setting itself, and what is unique about it as an educational context. Nonformal education sites such as libraries, museums, parks, and zoos also serve as commons or third places for their communities (Harris, 2007; Oldenburg, 1999). Commons of old were "public space[s] that anchored the American vision of democracy" (Daloz, Keen, & Keen, 1996, p. 2). Even though historically certain groups have been marginalized from these public places, they are ideally places "where diverse parts of a community could come together and hold a conversation within a shared sense of participation and responsibility" (p. 2). Another related term to describe this phenomenon is third places, developed in the field of sociology to make sense of informal public life. These places are public locations, such as cafes, bars, and bookstores that meet the human need to connect with others in places that are neither work nor home (Oldenburg, 1989). The first place is the home, the second is the work setting, and the third are places that bring "together communities of interest to peruse, discuss, debate, and celebrate the world of learning and the creative arts" (Demas & Scherer, 2002, p. 67). A good example of a third place is public libraries, which belong to the entire community and have increasingly become places for social interaction. Many libraries and other nonformal institutions set aside spaces for people to gather. These places become "a place different from home or work, a place where people can come to learn, think, explore, play, reflect and socialize" (Harris, 2007, p. 146). They are seen as places that facilitate social capital and civic virtue, which emerge from reciprocal productive social relations within a community. Third places, or commons, are seen as helping build communities by promoting trust, tolerance, and cooperation by providing places for fostering of social networks (Taylor, Parrish, & Banz, 2010).

Commons are also locations of contestation, spaces "where

cultures meet, clash, and grapple with each other, often in contexts of highly asymmetrical relations of power" (Pratt, 2001, p. 4). Nonformal education programs, particularly museums, can face public backlash in response to certain events for disrupting main-stream narratives of the larger American story (Taylor, Parrish, & Banz, 2010). An example is the controversy associated with the ex-hibit of the Enola Gay airplane at the Smithsonian Institution. It pre-sented the dropping of the atomic bomb on Hiroshima from mul-tiple perspectives (Yakel, 2000). Other examples of contestation play out in libraries across the country every September during Banned Books Week, reminding patrons of their constitutional rights "to both seek and receive information from all points of view without restriction" (Intellectual Freedom Basics, 2009, p. 3). This contesta-tion is a by-product of a clash of competing narratives that emerge as learners and educators, shaped by their own positionalities, inter-act within the larger and dominant narrative located in the nonformal education program.

CONCLUSION

From a review of the literature it is apparent that what is known about nonformal education has made great strides over the last 40 years. As sites of learning and teaching, nonformal education is ubiquitous in the cultural landscape, often easily accessible and decentralized. It serves a significant role in promoting lifelong learn-ing in society. These sites far surpass formal institutions of learning in number and variety. Nonformal education challenges scholars to take a more active role in better understanding how these sites pro-mote learning and what role adult educators can play in facilitating learning, both on personal and social levels. Despite this growing understanding, we need to move beyond these simple constructions of practice and focus on the complexity of teaching in nonformal settings. This involves investigating teaching as it plays out in the nonformal setting. It also means asking: How does the nonformal setting shape the educators and their practice? How do nonformal educators engage learners who enter this setting with varied inter-est, motivations, and expectations? How do educators manage the multiple stories that an institution represents and the multiple beliefs held by learners? These questions and others remind the reader of the complex nature of teaching within nonformal settings and highlight the significant differences from what is found when teaching in more formal settings.

CHAPTER 3

How the Nonformal Setting Shapes Practice

On an early chilly fall morning in eastern Pennsylvania, a group of bird-watchers is beginning to congregate at a nature park for a guided hike. There are 10 adults loosely gathered wearing thick jackets, gloves, and binoculars around their necks, and many are carrying bird lists in their pockets and backpacks. Some stand alone, while others are in small groups as they wait for the arrival of the park educator, Betty. Most of the adults don't seem to know each other, conversation is at minimum, although there is some discussion overheard about how surprised they are to see others up this early in the morning in such cold weather. As Betty arrives, she signals everyone to join her at the trailhead. She is particularly excited about this walk, because there is a good chance that today they will see hawks migrating south. The group gathers loosely in a semicircle facing the educator. As she scans the participants, she doesn't see any familiar faces and realizes that she has little idea of the learners' abilities at bird identification.

Furthermore, Betty also notices many are stamping their feet to keep warm, and there seems to be a range of expressions reflecting varying levels of interest and desire to begin the walk. Also, she remembers from past experience that she is likely to have little time with this group, as the interest level of most learners on these walks lasts about 45-75 minutes, based on the degree of bird activity and the weather conditions in the park. As time and the chill in the air bear down on the park educator, she thinks about this unfamiliar group of learners, and questions come to her mind: What do I need to be aware of about this nonformal setting that will have a significant influence on the outcome of this experience? How will this particular setting shape my teaching and also influence the learning experience of the participants? What can I do to maximize the power of this setting and minimize its challenges? These questions and others will frame the following discussion, focusing particularly on the unique nonformal setting and how it impacts practice.

A way to understand the nature of the nonformal setting is to begin with thinking about the vignette of the park educator. Betty faces challenges that are unique to teaching in nonformal settings and are often less of an issue in more formal educational settings. Those that come to mind that are most obvious, such as distractions from the weather and other wildlife (Bitgood, 2002; Taylor, 2005; Taylor & Caldarelli, 2004), the diversity found among learners in their knowledge of bird watching, age, education, and social background (Busque, 1991; Falk, Koran, & Dierking, 1986), and time constraints (Taylor, 2006). Other factors less obvious and equally influential include the nature of participation (voluntary participation, free choice) (Falk, 2001; Falk & Dierking, 2002); the novel setting (Bitgood, 2002), and informal learning (Bitgood, 2002). Further, it will become apparent as the discussion unfolds that several factors impact learners and educators most significantly on an emotional level, influencing how and to what degree they engage in the nonformal learning experience. The unique nature of the setting potentially stimulates a wide range of emotions. "There is both professional opinion and empirical research which suggest that the major advantages of learning activities in nonformal settings over those in formal settings may lie in the affective domain" (Meredith, Fortner, & Mullins, 1997, p. 806).

Often the intensity of the emotional experience captures and holds the learners' interest. However the educator needs to provide more than a stimulating experience. Events often require interpretation, an awareness of its complexity and nuance, without which the learners can easily lose interest or become distracted. The more nonformal educators are aware of these contextual factors, how they manifest, how they relate to each other, their practical implications and their emotional impact on the learners, the more control educators will have over their practice. Below, contextual factors are discussed in greater depth, more fully articulating its influence on the nonformal educational experience.

DISTRACTIONS

Distractions are inherent in any teaching situation, although in nonformal settings they are often more pronounced. The nonformal "environment is flooded with competing stimuli, many of them distracting the learner from focusing on a single educational message" (Bitgood, 2002, p. 461). On the other hand, in formal settings, such as a classroom, the instructional environment is set up purposefully to minimize distractions and foster conditions so that the attention of the learners is focused on the instructor.

Any significant distraction in a nonformal setting generally tends to be more intense emotionally and often acts as competing stimuli to the educator and the focus of the learning. Furthermore, educators often cannot completely remove distractions. Instead, it is more a matter of providing a stronger stimulus that keeps the learners focused on them, and not the distraction. They have to become astute at planning for, developing an awareness of, and finding ways to respond in order to minimize distractions in a timely fashion.

A number of examples illustrate the significance of distractions and how they impact practice. For example, the bird-watching experience on a chilly early morning would challenge any educator to keep the participants focused on the task ahead, more on the birds and less on trying to stay warm. In addition to the cold, the park itself is often replete with other distractions, such as the possibility of seeing other wildlife, inclement weather, varying conditions of the trail, and meeting other hikers.

In this particular case, one approach I observed was the initial reminder before the hike to be prepared for the possibility of inclement weather. This was followed by a brief discussion facilitated by the educator as the group spotted a particular bird. She made a point to keep the group moving up the trail until the sun started to rise higher in the sky, warming the day. Although not observed, it might be possible to bring along a large thermos of coffee to share at resting points on the trail.

Similar kinds of distractions were found when observing the consumer self-help clinics in the home improvement retail stores. The clinics were often located in a major thoroughfare of the store, and the participants and instructor were at times distracted by people briefly stopping to observe the clinic. In addition, the store message system blared intermittently in the background, along with other loud noises common in such large and cavern-like retail buildings. In response to these distractions, the instructors often did the obvious by talking louder. More subtle approaches were also used that were equally effective. Referring to the clinic in Chapter 1 about changing a faucet, the instructor made a particular point to place on a table in front of the learners an array of interesting tools and plumbing ware relevant to changing a faucet. This piqued the learners' interest. The customers of the store were also given opportunities to handle the tools and ask questions about them. This often acted as a stronger stimulus than any of the other distractions in the surrounding environment.

Nonformal educators will need to be prepared for distractions that are inherent to their teaching environment. They must plan accordingly by providing stimuli that will maintain the learners' interest and minimize distractions. An advantage the educator often has that helps maintain the learners' interest is the novel setting, and how the educator maximizes its significance for the learner.

LEARNER HETEROGENEITY

Learner heterogeneity is indicative of the wide range of differences such as ability, age, race, class, gender, and sexual orientation found in most nonformal education events. The differences that tend to be most influential and challenging for the educator are age and ability such as prior knowledge of the educational experience. For example, concerning age, I observed an interpretive nature hike led one evening at a local city park. There were close to 30 participants, with an age range that spanned almost 60 years from the youngest at 4-5 years old to the oldest at 70-80 years old. A wide age range implies an equally significant variation in the knowledge and abilities of the participants. Equally challenging for the guide were not only the wide range of abilities but also the varying levels of interest on this interpretive hike.

Before discussing how to respond to this challenge, it is important to recognize that despite the high degree of learner heterogeneity, some aspects of the group will work in favor of helping the educator. Most of these learners chose to attend, therefore it is likely their interest and motivation were already piqued as the hike began. Also, they were, in this case, able to leave at any time, if they became disinterested or felt that a hike under these conditions was not ideal. Furthermore, a nonformal setting often offers stimuli that if properly engaged will assist the educator in capturing and maintaining the interest of the learners.

Keeping in mind the high motivation of the learners and the power of the nonformal setting, the educators in most of the cases were observed using similar strategies that helped address the challenge associated with learner heterogeneity. One strategy was assessing the learners at the beginning of the event. For example, during the tours of the museum, I observed docents having casual conversations with museum visitors prior to the beginning of the tour. The docents used these conversations to assess the visitors' interest, to decide on how the tour might be modified (if at all) to better suit those interests, and, most significantly, to establish a rapport.

In another example, at a home improvement clinic about laying wood flooring, the instructor, Sam, began by asking participants standing around the table about their particular flooring needs. Usually the needs centered around the location of where the flooring was going to be laid in the home, the type of flooring desired, and the skills required to complete the task. Following questioning, Sam would attempt to address those particular needs as he covered the clinic material. By assessing the learners prior to initiating the session, the educator was better prepared to make the clinic relevant.

TIME CONSTRAINTS

Time is a significant factor for the learner and their learning. Attention and curiosity are fleeting phenomena particularly in free choice settings, where learners will easily disengage mentally from a presentation and move on to other activities they find more interesting. The length of the educational activities I observed fell between 25 and 75 minutes. Even though these times are short, there are also physiological factors, such as the consequence of standing in one location for an extended period of time. This can be challenging for the learner as well as the educator. If as an event, such as a tour, is not emotionally engaging in promoting curiosity and attention and runs over a long period of time, learners will feel bored (yawning) and restless (shuffling feet). This was particularly the case among learners I observed in the home improvement store clinics. Standing on a hard concrete floor in one place for more than 20 minutes starts to prove challenging, particularly for middle-aged and older learners. Since the learners are here by their own choosing, it becomes imperative for the educator to provide a stimulating instructional experience that keeps the learners focused on the clinic and not on their feet. So, as learners become antsy and begin to shuffle their feet, these behaviors are indicators of learners' emotions and levels of interest in relationship to the educational event. If properly appraised and addressed in a timely manner by the educator, the situation can often be rectified, resulting in a more successful educational experience.

Another time constraint is the limited opportunity to engage the learner beyond one educational experience. Basically, most of these instructors will never see the same learners twice, particularly in relationship to the same educational topic. In essence, each time educators initiate an education activity or clinic, the learners are new to them, and they have likely never met before. In multiple observations of home improvement clinics, park, and museum education events at the same location, I never saw the same learners twice. In response the educators have to find ways to quickly develop a rapport with the learners. How educators handled this effectively is discussed in Chapter 4.

NOVEL SETTING

The nonformal setting is often new, unique, and possibly a setting the learner has not entered before. This experience is quite different from the formal classroom, where the emphasis is about sameness, homogeneity, and standardization. Furthermore, the novel stimuli often is visual in nature and less verbal, another distinction from formal settings where there is greater emphasis on the spoken word (Bitgood, 2002). Novelty also sheds light on the relationship between emotions and learning in a nonformal setting. This is particularly the case in museums, historical sites, parks, and other cultural institutions where there are opportunities to learn in the original setting or a close fabrication of the original setting. These settings can be described as having an authentic presence. The emotional power of such a setting is brought to life by Courtenay's (1995) description of his visit to the Sixth Floor Museum in Dallas, the actual location where Oswald shot President Kennedy:

> It is an authentic context for learning. . . . There is no gainsaying of the profundity of the emotion you experience as, unrestrained by person or barrier, you approach one of a number of windows which affords a would-be assassin barely interrupted visual passage to the street and plaza below. (p. 4)

The more novel and reflective the original setting, the more likely the context speaks for itself. Here the educator potentially plays more of an adjunct role, interpreting and highlighting key contextual cues to maximize the emotive nature of the experience.

A good example of the power of a novel nonformal experience and how it captures the attention of the learner and minimizes the role of the docent was observed when I toured a famous craftsman's home and workshop in eastern Pennsylvania. The home itself was an artistic expression and as you entered the first floor where his workshop was located, immediately your senses were overwhelmed. The room was filled with beautifully designed furniture and wooden sculptures reflecting flawless symmetry. Almost every piece including a desk, chairs, tables and steps to the second floor was constructed by hand. Not only were the learners visually stimulated, but they were also allowed to touch most anything in the room. Both the visual and physical aspects spoke so powerfully that the docent, in this case Andrea, could move to the edge of the learning experience. When I interviewed docents from this site, they spoke of this very phenomenon without being prompted. For example, Andrea exclaimed about the site: "[It] doesn't need me. It doesn't need anybody. All anybody has to do is walk in that space and go 'Wow'." Similarly, Bernice commented, "I could shut up the whole time and just be in the room."

However, for other locations, I found that docents were central to fostering the novel setting, the feeling of being there, by bringing objects and the uniqueness of the place to life for the learner. For example, on a tour of a historic tavern and owner's home I observed many visitors looking in a curious way at an unusual white cone-like object on a vertical spool located on a dining room table. Eventually Marcus, a docent dressed in period clothing, explained that this object was sugar, hard packed for storage in that time period. Once he pointed this out, along with other objects, the visitors were pulled closer into an authentic experience of the setting. As Phil, an interpretive guide for the tavern, explained, "I have to be on the site to show them the actual artifacts." Without this explanation, the learner would likely overlook the novelty of the object or other unique aspects of the setting.

For nonformal educators it is essential that they highlight the novelty of the setting for the learners, even though for the educator it obviously is no longer a novel experience. Furthermore, the educator needs to be comfortable at times not being at the center of attention, but moving to the margins and letting the setting take center stage.

VOLUNTARY PARTICIPATION

One of the most significant contextual factors of teaching in public places that is often not discussed in the adult education literature is the influence of voluntary participation, and how it helps further the distinction from teaching in formal education. Another way to understand voluntary participation is through a discussion of "free choice" education (Falk, 2001; Falk & Dierking, 2002). Free choice is where the learner has the choice to attend or not attend (physically and mentally) an educational event, as well as the choice to leave at any time. In the bird-watching experience discussed earlier, the participants had the choice to attend in the first place, and often the choice to leave as long as it would be safe for them to walk the trail on their own, return to their cars, and leave the park. In more formal settings, often individuals don't have a choice or permission to attend an education event due to age limits, cost, and admission criteria. Withdrawing from a formal event often has greater consequences such as cost (loss of tuition) and outcome of performance indicators (failing grade).

A way to understand the significance of this factor is through a metaphor of the "power of feet." The power of feet is the power garnered or held by the learners as a byproduct of voluntary participation within a public location. The ease of the learners to enter and exit the nonformal site shifts some control of the learning experience from the teacher to the learners and puts greater pressure on the educator to maintain the interest of the learners.

Although withdrawing from nonformal events by learners was observed in park sites less often, because of walking alone in the outdoors, it still took place. I saw how voluntary participation drastically changes the size of a group, noted during an observation of an evening guided interpretive walk at local city park, "At the beginning of the walk there were 29 learners, adults and children present. . . . Within an hour almost a third of the group had left."

Voluntary participation at home improvement clinics took on another level of complexity. Learners withdrew at various times during the clinic and new learners often joined after the clinic had already begun. It was not unusual to observe late arrivals asking questions similar to what had already been addressed. This exit and entry of learners at various times demanded of the educator the ability to respond to new interest and, at the same time, maintain a commitment to the interest of those learners who had entered the clinic at the beginning. During a clinic on how to lay ceramic tile I recorded, "At the scheduled time of the clinic at least five learners were present. . . . Ten minutes into the clinic the group had doubled in size. . . . At the end of the clinic there were six learners."

In response to the "power of feet" the nonformal educator must regularly appraise the learners' emotive states, checking for their levels of interest, much more so than would be expected within a formal educational setting, where often the teacher has a "captured" audience. The goal is to "[attract] the attention of the visitor and [hold] attention long enough to communicate its intended message" (Meredith, Fortner, and Mullins, 1997, p. 808). In addition, once the learners are involved, there needs to be continual awareness or appraisal of the learners' attention level. Otherwise the educator will have little understanding of how to respond if and when the learners' interest dissipates, and why they might choose to leave the educational event. Consequently, the presence of free choice potentially creates anxiety, particularly in less experienced educators, compromising cognition and limiting the available mental resources to respond to the myriad of everyday educational challenges (Eysenck & Calco, 1992).

CONCLUSION

This chapter describes the uniqueness of the nonformal setting and the role it plays in shaping both teaching and learning. The more educators can be aware of how the ever-present distractions, the wide heterogeneity of learners, the time constraints, the novel settings, and the voluntary participation shape practice, the more control they have in facilitating a successful nonformal educational experience. The challenge is developing this awareness of what to look for when planning, teaching, and nonformal educational experiences. To help the educator in developing the awareness of contextual factors that shape practice, Chapter 5 describes a guiding reflexive framework.

CHAPTER 4

Instructional Approaches

It was afternoon on a warm sunny Sunday at a small private historic home of a famous artist who worked in wood sculpture, prints, and furniture. A curator, Bernie, was preparing to lead a tour. Eight people gathered in a nearby gift shop, a remodeled garage near the artist's home, waiting for the tour to begin. Bernie was introducing himself to each visitor, finding out what brought each of them to the home and where they were from. The gift shop offered examples of authentic work of the artist and provided a staging point for the tour. This implicitly set the context and raised expectations of what was in store.

As the tour began, Bernie gathered the learners outside, providing both a visual and textual overview of the home, and what it reflected about the artist's work and life. He also presented a brief history and background of the artist. Embedded in his narrative was personal information about the artist, illustrating a human face for the learners, before they entered the home. This beginning narrative provided a framework from which the tour emerged and a context to give greater meaning and appreciation of the artist's work. Finally, before the group started to move toward the entrance, Bernie set some ground rules and expectations, both about how the learners should engage the art and about the tour itself. In this particular case, unusually so, learners were allowed to touch anything, unless noted, and they were also encouraged to ask questions at any time on the tour.

After the opening presentation, Bernie led the group to the back entrance. As the tour progressed he would stop at predetermined points, unless directed elsewhere by a learner, and identify something in particular about the home itself, a sculpture, or a piece of furniture. He often described the work or some aspect of the home through a short story of what was going on in the artist's life or what might have provided the impetus for a particular work. At times these stories would be humorous and out of the ordinary, making the tour interesting and engaging. Also, it was apparent that the tour was organized in a purposeful manner to keep the learners attentive, by making sure at each stage or room of the home an unusual work was presented. For example, in the main studio was an extraordinary desk that had variety of surprising features. Bernie selected one learner to explore the desk, demonstrating its wonderment by opening drawers and hidden cabinets, while the others observed, giving everyone a direct experience with the object.

Despite the inherent structure of the tour, on the surface it seemed fluid and generally spontaneous, particularly because learners were free to roam within a particular room of the home and not held together as a group by Bernie's presentation. He spoke only to those that gave him their attention, letting others wander where their interests took them. Yet, the learners seemed to be always under his gaze, both for protecting the artist's work and for observing their reactions and interest level.

As the tour progressed through the small home and studio, Bernie seemed quite attentive to the learners' interests, by both addressing questions that were raised and watching where their interests took them. For example, when he saw someone giving particular attention to a piece of furniture crafted by the artist, he would integrate a discussion about it into the tour script, as if it was part of the tour all along. After about 45-60 minutes, the tour ended in the foyer of the main entrance of the home.

This brief vignette, like others in the book, provides a backdrop from which to reflect and identify various teaching approaches found within a nonformal educational setting. These methods include both learner-centered and teacher-centered approaches. They include an emphasis on visual demonstration and hands-on opportunities, storytelling, minimal learner expectations, promoting fun and entertainment, and fostering affective learning. These approaches emerged from the research I conducted at three different nonformal sites: stores, parks, and museums. It is important to note that when and how often these instructional approaches are used is determined by the unique setting, institutional expectations, and educator preferences. Also, as the discussion demonstrates, teaching in nonformal settings is much more complex than has previously been reported in the literature.

VISITOR-CENTERED APPROACH

The visitor-centered or learner-centered facilitative approach has long been considered inherent to nonformal education. This means that the educational experience is centered and framed within the interest of the visitor or learner. The term *visitor* was chosen because most nonformal education programming is less intensive, where the learners briefly engage or visit the education experience and a learner-centered approach is not the dominant approach to teaching.

Often the learner-centered approach has been anecdotally described within the context of a non-hierarchical relationship reported to exist between the learner and facilitator (Ahmed & Coombs, 1975; Marsick & Watkins, 1990). Yet, from the description of the tour of the historic home led by Bernie, it would be difficult to conclude that the experience was predominantly learner-centered.

To understand where this approach emerges requires looking below the surface at the less obvious. The visitor-centered approach is seen in a subtle manner by the docents, park guides, or consumer educators, most often at the beginning of the nonformal education experience, where they make an effort to connect the nonformal experience with the learners' interests. For example, Bernie made a particular point to find out what brought the learners to the historic home. With that information, he often finds a way to connect specifically to their interest if the opportunity arises. He stated that at the beginning of tours "I try to make sure I know where they're from . . . That will gear the way I present my tour." In other museums I observed a similar approach to find out if the learners were from the nearby community or from out of state. The learners' place of residence would determine to some extent how much background was presented about the local area surrounding the historic site.

Others would see this approach as a means of assessing the knowledge level of the participants. For example, Harvey, who gave clinics on seasonal planting at a local home improvement store, saw himself as a facilitator, and described his approach: "to feel out the crowd, and find out what their interests are, what they're gonna see, and build upon that." This was similar to Betty, a naturalist at a state park, who explained:

> By engaging the audience, you find out what people know. . . . If they don't know much at all, or have a lot of misconceptions . . . then you can address that. It's also part of what keeps people connected and interested in what you're talking about and getting information back from them. It's sort of like, "Oh, this leader is interested in what I know."

Others would go even further, particularly in the case of the park educators. Many of them saw it important not only to assess the learners' interest and knowledge level, but also to help people feel safe in a new environment. Through building a rapport with the learners, a visitor-centered approach helped those who were less confident in the wilderness feel more secure and comfortable. For instance, Jan, a park guide, stated, "People aren't going to interact with nature, aren't going to feel comfortable with it. . . . So the main thing is being comfortable outside . . . and the more they know, the more comfortable they feel."

Although the visitor-centered approach is not an approach that frames the entire teaching experience, the idea of connecting with learner's needs and interests is important when working in the nonformal settings, maybe more so than in formal settings. Time is fleeting and the educator has to find a quick way to establish a connection with the learner.

TRANSMISSION-CENTERED APPROACH

Often seen in opposition to the visitor-centered approach is the educator's reliance on a teacher-centered, transmission, or expert approach to teaching. This model of teaching is defined as:

> The most 'traditional' and long-standing perspective on teaching. It is based on the belief that a relatively stable body of knowledge and/or procedure can be efficiently transmitted to

learners. The primary focus is on efficient and accurate delivery of that body of knowledge to learners. (Pratt & Associates, 1998, pp. 39-40)

Looking back on Bernie's experience, this transmission approach was evident throughout the tour of the historic home in his sharing important stories and facts about the artist's home. Furthermore, it is how many nonformal educators understand their role as teachers. They are the expert and their purpose is to share what they know about objects in the museums, the plant life in a forest, or the various tools used to change a faucet. It is this expertise that is central in much of nonformal education, and it a primary reason why people attend these events. For example, Steve, a naturalist, described his practice when teaching in a natural setting:

> Conveying my knowledge to people who are interested in that particular topic. . . . It's people who want knowledge on a particular topic that show up at a program. Basically, I just try to think of what kind of information they're looking for and present that information to them.

The transmission approach in the nonformal setting comes across as content driven and at times seems highly scripted. Here, knowledge is seen as external from the learner and something transferred to them by the educator. For example, Sam describes his role when doing a clinic on flooring in a local home improvement store: "I try to get out as much information as I can." Also, indicative of this orientation, park educators rely heavily on text and often spend hours reading materials in preparation for an interpretive hike or bird walk. For instance, Sarah, a naturalist, discussed her emphasis on the importance of understanding the content prior to leading a walk. She stated:

> For this particular walk, I do a lot of research at night, so I've read throughout all different kinds of programs. Whenever somebody would ask me a question, if I didn't have the answer, I'd go look it up, and then I'd read a little bit further than that in case the next question was a little bit more advanced.

Despite the appearance of an emphasis on content by the educators, like visitor-centered teaching, at times a more nuanced facilitative practice is operating just below the surface. For example, even though consumer educators were provided with a written script for each clinic by the home improvement retailer, they rarely adhered to the script and sometimes questioned its content. Eric, who provides clinics on faux painting, stated:

> I'm gonna teach what I find that works regardless of what somebody on paper puts down. . . . I find that with crackle glaze, for instance, the manufacturer says, "Let it dry a half-hour to forty-five minutes." Well, I found if you let it dry forty-five minutes, it's not going to . . . be as effective.

Similarly, museum educators spoke of not using scripts, and felt that there was freedom to choose different subtopics to emphasize and give greater attention to what interested the learners on a tour. As Bernice stated: "I don't like to be scripted." What Eric, Bernie, and other nonformal educators are saying is that despite the importance of transferring information and an emphasis on content preparation, they desire some definitive control over constructing their presentations.

This constructivist approach to shaping a presentation embedded within a transmission model manifested itself in a variety of ways. One example was seen through the role of storytelling. The use of storytelling converts the didactic and factual presentation into a narrative, stimulating greater interest among learners. It builds upon the unique approach of each educator. For instance, as Sarah stated: "I try to make the facts into an interesting story. It's not really a story, but it is more than a string of facts." Furthermore the storytelling is seen as personal, with each educator deciding to some extent what to share and how it is told to learners. Quinn, a volunteer docent, stated: "you've got to come up with the story you want to tell, the overall story."

This individually constructed presentation is further complicated by where the educator gathers knowledge to construct their "story." For the park educators and museum docents, the knowledge of presentations emerged predominantly from texts such as field guides, and historic books. Each educator uniquely constructs the stories. The consumer educator, on the other hand, rarely relied on text. Here the presentation and reconstruction of the presentation were rooted in personal experience with a particular skill, for example plumbing or painting. An explanation for this difference is that most consumer educators have a trades background. They most likely learned the related skills through a direct hands-on experience and therefore are likely to draw on that experience as opposed to the text.

Like the visitor-centered approach, the transmission approach is modified and situated based on the public setting, the topic being presented, and the experience of the educator. It is not simply a presentation of facts. It is a constructed presentation, at times a story, unique to each educator and constantly reconstructed based on the needs and interests of the learners. Also, as we will see next, the educator does not exclusively construct the nonformal educational event. Others are also involved.

ENCOURAGING QUESTIONS APPROACH

In combination with the presentation of information or stories, the other primary instructional approach used by many nonformal educators is encouraging learners to ask questions. The number of questions and resulting interaction is often seen as an indicator to measure the success of the educational experience. Looking back on Bernie's tour, he began like most who teach in nonformal settings, by encouraging questions from the learners. Others go even further. For example, Jim, an environmental educator at a local bird sanctuary, discussed a hike he led at night by moonlight. He saw questioning as both an expectation and a responsibility of the learners. He stated: "I hope they ask questions. . . . 'Okay, well, how do you move at night?' and, 'How is it different than the day?'" Similarly, Andrea, the docent at the craftsman's home, had the same expectations. She stated: "I expect them to ask a lot of questions and I hope that they will."

Questions were seen as the primary means for engaging the

audience and also as a measure of the learners' interests in the tour. For instance, Phil, an interpretive guide, said: "If they're interested enough in what we are saying, then they have questions . . . We'd try to get the questions out of them if we possibly could." Fostering questions from learners, often a big desire, poses a challenge for most educators.

One strategy, previously discussed, stresses the importance of asking questions of learners, assessing their interests, and paying close attention to what they gravitate toward on a tour or a walk. For instance, as Bernie watched learners spend time with a particular sculpture, he asked them: "What do you think the object is?" By initiating a discussion, hopefully greater interaction would follow. Asking questions of learners helps create an atmosphere for interaction to evolve between the guide and the learners. Also, I noticed that the nonformal educators who allowed for brief periods of silence seemed to have more questions from their learners.

Questioning also plays a role in constructing what is presented in the nonformal experience. To some degree questions determine what is going to be addressed or discussed on a tour, particularly in cultural institutions where there are often too many stories and too much information to be covered in one tour. What gets covered on a tour is shaped to some extent by what the learners ask the educator. For example, in a tour of an industrial museum, Rob, the docent, was observed handling a barrage of questions about how a large piece of machinery worked. Many questions brought to light information that would not have normally been discussed by Rob. As a consequence of the time constraints, less time was spent on other aspects of the museum. It was determined later that the reason for all these questions was that several of the learners had a personal connection with that particular machine during an earlier time in their lives. In fact some of them knew more about this machinery than the docent. Having this information in advance can help prepare the guide as the tour evolves.

The challenge for educators when it comes to questioning is learning ways to foster interaction with the learner and, at the same time, maintain the integrity of the educational experience. Those that seem the most successful are generally well prepared and knowledgeable. They recognize that the quality of information shared is much more important than the quantity. It is important to encourage questions and allow time for learner engagement.

EXPERIENTIAL APPROACH

Experiential teaching, as a pedagogical term, is used here in a very broad sense. It includes hands-on activities, such as handling objects and participating in programs in nonformal settings, particularly in cultural institutions such as museums and parks. It also describes an educator's often highly demonstrative and visual approach to teaching. Looking back at Bernie's tour sheds light on the experiential emphasis of his teaching. Most obvious was the visual significance of the tour, highlighting the artwork, furniture, and the usual aspects of the artist's home. Yet the educator can't assume that if something is present that it is actually seen. Often it is the role of the educator to show the learners how to see or what to see in particular when viewing an object or a setting.

This visual emphasis was also evident in the consumer education clinics located in the home improvement stores. Each clinic was organized with a strong emphasis on the visual and on making the course materials and products accessible to the customer. A table was generally set up with the necessary tools, equipment, and construction materials in a manner for learners to easily see. Clinic participants were often encouraged to gather around the table so they were close, and the educator could show and demonstrate the various items and, at times, pass them through the group for everyone to handle. For instance, Oscar, a professional plumber and part-time employee at a home improvement store, stressed the importance of this visual approach. He stated:

> I'm standing there saying: 'You take a faucet and put it in a sink,' No way! You have to have the show-and-tell thing. You need to see to make it work. . . . A lot of times when I'm showing people stuff or I'm working with [someone] one-on-one, I will take the stuff out of the pack and assemble it for them right in front of them.

The visual often coincides or is complemented with some form of hands-on opportunity. In Bernie's tour the learners were allowed to actually feel the wood sculptures in the artist's home. A consumer educator, Larry, who offered a workshop on recess lighting, stated: "Letting that person touch, feel what they're doing, walk them through it so that they get a better understanding for it instead of just sitting in a classroom and looking up on the chalk board . . . you're able to retain it better."

Hands-on is not just about the physical touch. It is also recognizing that greater involvement by the learners leads to more significant learning. For example, for John, who often leads interpretive hikes, it is matter of providing opportunities for learners to actively engage the natural environment. He stated: "If you do something that the people can actually participate in rather than just listening, if they can become active participants in something, I think their experience is much better and they will tend to learn a little more."

The visual and, at times, hands-on experiences guided by an educator are a central, although often overlooked characteristic of nonformal education. Yet just because learners are able to view something doesn't mean they are seeing and understanding in a way that the educator intends. Often they need help in interpretation, in how to view a particular object or place.

MINIMAL EXPECTATIONS

Nonformal educators usually have a minimal level of expectations for learners. Several reasons explain this. Learners in most cases have the discretion to leave, and other times enter an educational experience after it has already begun. Another overarching factor, which highlights a major difference between nonformal education and more formal settings, is the lack of effort, formal or otherwise, to measure or gauge learner outcomes. This is not to say there aren't any expectations at all. They tended however to focus predominantly on the learners' actions and reactions during the education experience. For some educators, it was an expectation of being engaged and asking questions.

Those educators that expressed the least expectations of learners were consumer educators, who seemed to have some difficulty with this concept. It was as if they hadn't ever thought of having any expectations of their learners. Expectations were so minimal largely because learners had such ease of access in and out of the clinics. For example, Eric, who was giving a clinic on painting, stated: "They should be willing and want to know what's going on . . . that just gives me more information as a facilitator to custom tailor the clinic. As far as if I expect them to go and buy something, no, I don't." Moving along the continuum, park educators raised the bar a bit by reminding learners to respect the natural environment, minimizing the impact of the hike or walk. I observed them at times reminding learners to stay on the trail or avoid certain areas. Also, if the hike posed some physical risk or other safety issues, like during the "moonwalk" discussed earlier, the educator would establish significant ground rules before the tour began.

Even though it generally wasn't an issue of safety, the expectations were raised even higher among docents in museums. Many saw themselves as stewards of the museum or historic site, expressing a strong sense of responsibility toward the site itself and the safety of the objects held. Most were passionate about their responsibility as custodians of the collections. For example, Bernice, a docent in the sculptor's home, remembered a learner opening a cabinet without requesting permission. She stated: "People can't just run off and just go open up cabinets and check things out. It makes me very nervous because I feel responsible. . . . My primary responsibility is to make sure that the integrity of the objects and their safety are guaranteed."

A possible consequence of minimal learner expectation held by the educator is that learners are likely to have less expectations as well about how much they can gain from the experience. For instance in the self-help consumer clinic, it is likely that the educator as well as the learners did not have high expectations of the experience. However, in experiences such as a hike in a park or a tour of a museum where the learner had to go to greater lengths to participate (e.g., cost, driving distance, and time commitment), expectations among both the educator and the learners likely increased.

PLANNING DRIVEN BY EXPERIENCE AND EXPERTISE

Planning in the area of nonformal education as an educational approach is rarely discussed, particularly from the perspective of the nonformal educator. If it is discussed, it is often seen as participatory, wherein the educator and the learners together decide on what and how the experience is going to unfold. This view of planning is rooted in a learner-centered conception of teaching. In these case studies a learner-centered approach tells only a small part of the story of planning in a nonformal setting. Planning is more complex and varied than, for example, just briefly appraising the learners' interests prior to the beginning of an educational experience. In nonformal education, planning involves the following:

1.   What the educator believes is necessary to prepare and to think about prior to beginning the experience.
2.   What happens as the experience begins, such as developing a rapport with learners.
3.   What happens as the educational event unfolds.
4.   Evaluating the experience as it ends.

Also, in the case of this discussion what seems to shape planning most is the experience of the nonformal educator and the ongoing development of expertise.

For example, when it came to the consumer educators, most talked of engaging in little preparation prior to a clinic. A few even described the process as "winging it." For example, Harvey, who worked in the gardening center, stated: "Basically, I looked over the information a little bit. I figured I'd basically wing it like I did in high school. . . . I can talk about nothing for long periods of time." This minimal planning approach to a clinic seemed to be a product of personal experience. I observed that there was generally a cursory review of the script or curricular guide provided by the store, and more of a reliance on past work experience to provide the information necessary to conduct the clinic. Allen, a plumber, described his approach to planning: "There was a guideline they had printed out which I didn't really look through . . . [I] just dropped it aside because it didn't really help a whole lot." The clinics were often led by highly skilled trades people, like Allen, who had many years of experience with plumbing. Offering a clinic on changing a faucet, from his perspective, would require little planning. This was particularly the case for clinics that emphasized hands-on skills. It is important to note that those who had less personal experience and expertise with the home improvement clinic topic seemed to spend more time preparing, such as reviewing material prior to giving the clinic. This was particularly true of those programs that were less skill-based and instead required more recalling of semantic knowledge, such as types of and facts about plants in the nursery.

Nonformal education programs that focused more on sharing information and had less emphasis on skill demonstration required educators to think differently about planning. This was particularly the case among museum and park educators whose programs were more content driven in preparation for their education programs. For example, Dewey, a naturalist, discussed how he prepared for his bird-watching hikes. He stated:

> So as far as the content of the bird walks, depending on the time of the year, I may refresh myself for some field marks. The night before this, I was sitting down with my warbler book looking at plates just in case I see this bird tomorrow . . . I can tell this bird is different from this bird because of these characteristics.

A similar approach to planning was found among the tour guides at museums. Usually they had to spend much time studying, particularly if a novice, the history of a home or objects in preparation for a tour. They memorized a good deal of factual information, much more than they would ever have to share with the learners. However, over time, once they became well versed in the curriculum, less planning was required. Regardless, for most educators, planning was predominantly driven by how to be best prepared when sharing information. There was such an emphasis on being knowledgeable about the topic, whether as a product of experience or through a lengthy preparation, that it seemed to take precedence over other issues related to teaching (e.g., rapport with learners, presentation skills, hands-on activities, promoting fun).

Along with the planning prior to the event, it was apparent that the educator needed to continually evaluate the original plan as the experience unfolded due to the ever-shifting nature of nonformal education. This need to regularly evaluate an educational plan is also important when teaching in other settings. In nonformal education, however, the need is heightened because of the unique contextual factors. These include the limited time to engage the learners and the ease with which learners can enter and leave the event. By regularly assessing the plan, determining what is working and what is not by appraising the state of the learner, the educator can rectify problems before the event is over and learners pursue other interests, expressing their free choice.

Finally, evaluation of the nonformal event also has its unique challenges. In most observed events, learners leave as quickly as they enter, making it difficult to gather formal or informal feedback. In the home improvement clinics, the retail store often provided a standard evaluation form to the learners for written feedback. I noticed few learners completing the form following the event. As the clinic ended, learners quickly dispersed, some leaving during the final questions, so feedback was minimal at best. In the other case studies, gathering formal feedback from learners was also something rarely seen. The context challenged the implementation of program evaluation and the need for feedback was not as great, which is consistent with the level of expectations often held by the educator for learners in these settings.

FUN AND GOOD HUMOR

Fundamental to nonformal education is the importance of providing an enjoyable and fun experience for the learners. What does "fun" mean in the nonformal setting? It reflects a number of characteristics, each observed to a greater or lesser extent based on the skills and confidence of the educator, such as informality, self-deprecating humor, jokes, and an air of general levity. The most obvious and self-evident forms of fun were found among the consumer educators. Their goal was to attract as many consumers as they could. Projecting a fun experience as consumers walked by helped draw them into the clinic. It also meant providing a presentation that demonstrated that a home improvement project could actually be an enjoyable experience, whatever it was (e.g., faux painting, garden-ing). For example, Evelyn, who worked in the nursery, stated:

> I make them laugh, interject a funny [comment] and I mock myself a lot. I'll make fun of myself because when I'm potting plants, I have dirt everywhere, and then I'll say, "well you can see I'm a messy Bessie . . . " It's not all cut and dry . . . what I call stiff shirt.

Some of the educators saw fun as the central criteria for a successful learning experience. For example, Jason, a docent at a historic site, stated: "For me a successful experience means they're going to have fun and they're going to learn something and those two things are not mutually exclusive. Actually I think they're related. I think when people learn stuff they have fun."

Fun is propagated through a sense of informality. Often educators were observed introducing themselves by their first name, and, in general, there wasn't much ritual or any tedious preparation to begin the educational experience. Furthermore, the content was generally accessible to a wide range of learners with various ability levels. If the learners wanted to raise the bar, they would ask a more challenging question, which in turn would lead to a more involved discussion. For instance, John, the naturalist, stated: "With interpretive programs, you're more or less interpreting what you see. You aren't dealing with heavy duty concepts. Formal education is more purposeful and predetermined."

Essentially, what is important in creating a fun and enjoyable experience is recognizing the power of the affective (emotions) in the nonformal learning experience. Providing a fun experience fosters positive emotions. Engaging such feelings advantages the nonformal setting in learning. As noted, the skilled educator knows how to make the most of the setting and creates an experience that engages the emotions of the learner in positive ways.

CONCLUSION

Looking back over these various instructional approaches emphasizes the complexity of the nonformal educator's practice. They highlight the importance of being aware of how little the traditional anecdotal descriptors, such as learner-centered, accurately capture what is happening in these unique educational settings. The challenge for the educator is deciding, for example, when to share information or encourage questions, and how much of both. Also, when to raise or lower the expectations of the learners. How much time should be spent on planning? What should be the focus of the planning—studying the content or developing activities to better engage the learners? To help with these questions and others, the educator needs a reflective approach to nonformal education. This approach is discussed in Chapter 5.

CHAPTER 5

Teaching With Your Eyes Wide Open

At this point in the book it is important to explore how to make sense of nonformal education in practice. In other words, how do you make decisions in planning an educational experience? How do you decide what to do as the teaching event is unfolding? And, what should you think about after it is over? This chapter is an effort to encourage a reflective approach to teaching by taking into account what you have learned from the previous chapters and your prior teaching experience as you make decisions about teaching in nonformal settings. It also provides a model of teaching regardless of the nonformal situation.

One way to begin this reflective process is to spend a bit of time thinking about the three teaching vignettes described in Chapters 1, 3, and 4. Imagine yourself as an educator in each one of those settings. You are the plumber standing in the middle of a thoroughfare in large retail home improvement store teaching an ever-changing group of consumers how to fix a leaky faucet. Or, you are a park naturalist leading a group of adults on an interpretive hike at a state preserve near your home. Or, you are a docent providing a tour at a local historic site within your community. What comes to mind as you prepare yourself to begin these different educational endeavors? What do you see as important for teaching effectively in these settings? What do you think you will find most challenging about the setting, the visitors, and the curriculum? How do you prepare for the task ahead? How do you decide which teaching approaches you are going to use? What do you see as essential in your approach to teaching to help ensure a successful experience?

To respond effectively to these questions and others, educators must be aware of the complexity of the nonformal setting in relationship to their own approach to teaching. This awareness will allow the educators to teach with their eyes wide open. The means by which educators acquire this awareness is by reflecting on the nonformal situation and the underlying assumptions that support their teaching. This is a continuous process of reviewing past experience in relationship to what is happening in practice. It is a self-regulated process where educators are regularly studying their teaching and determining what is working and what is not. Through a reflective practice nonformal educators do not shoot from the hip when teaching (Schön, 1987). Instead, they are purposeful and informed when preparing, planning, and engaging in teaching. Teaching in a nonformal setting presents a limited opportunity to engage the learner, therefore it is imperative to make the most of what little time is available. The goal is teaching with a commitment to continually improve practice.

A reflective practice is not a new concept, but it is something that has rarely been discussed in relationship to teaching in nonformal settings. Reflective educators are more likely to understand their own practice and how it shapes a nonformal education experience. On other hand, non-reflective educators are at the whim of circumstance when teaching and are often unaware or unable to explain their practice and how it contributes to the success or lack of success of an educational event. For example, during a museum tour, I observed Rodney, a guide, talking at great length to a group of visitors. They had been standing for quite a while in one place, with little opportunity to take a rest or at least move to another part of the museum. Consequentially, there was a lot of shuffling of feet, antsy behavior, eyes wandering around the museum, and a growing lack of interest in the tour. All the while, Rodney did not seem to be aware of what was playing out in front of him. Instead he seemed more interested in sharing as much information as possible about the object in front of the visitors. Eventually, he stopped talking and moved the group to another station in the museum. After the tour was over, during the interview, the guide was asked to evaluate the success of the previous tour. Rodney concluded that, in general, the tour was a success, although he thought this group of visitors didn't seem as interested in the information being shared, particularly the interesting facts about the objects in the museum. When asked why he thought the visitors might not have been interested, he stated,

"Well you get groups like that now and then. They're just not into the tour, and there is not much you can do about it."

There clearly could be some truth to Rodney's statement about the learners, but regardless, it was apparent that he was not aware of his role in relationship to the tour experience. It was likely he wasn't very observant of the visitors and wasn't reflecting on his practice about what was working and not working, and why. He predominantly saw the lack of success resting on the shoulders of the learners and not himself. Furthermore, Rodney seemed to be teaching from rote, not from an awareness of practice. The more awareness educators have of their practice, the more control they have over the nonformal experience.

The reflective practice can be challenging for the educator, with so many things going on in a nonformal setting. To assist the educator in this task, there are four areas to focus on as a means to becoming more aware of the nonformal education experience and, more importantly, aware of what to think about when planning, engaging practice, and evaluating outcomes. The goal is to develop a deeper awareness of:

1. The two dominant roles of the nonformal educator.
2. The visitor as a learner.
3. The public versus private context in nonformal settings.
4. The institutional expectations.

In addition for quick reference, a set of reflective questions relevant to each area has been complied in a table at the end of this chapter (see Table 5.1).

THE TWO ROLES OF THE NONFORMAL EDUCATOR

The educator has primarily two competing roles while teaching in nonformal settings. One is that of an expert (teaching as transmission) and the other is a facilitator (visitor-centered teaching). The challenge is how to use these roles effectively and synergistically, based on the interest of the learners and the demands of the setting. The complementary and responsive use of these roles leads to a powerful interpretive nonformal experience for the learner.

As experts, most of the nonformal educators observed in the various sites were deeply versed in their topic. There was never enough time in one session for them to share everything they knew with the learners. In Chapter 4 Bernie was an example of an expert when he was giving a tour of a historic home. He knew a significant amount about the life of the artist who resided in the home, his work, and the home itself. Much of the time on the tour was spent with Bernie sharing pertinent information. It was his expertise and that of others that are often a major reason why people attend museum tours, spend time at home improvement clinics, and take guided interpretive hikes. When the educator is in the role of the expert, much of the time is spent talking to the audience and sharing information. This may seem like a simple task, but it is quite challenging to be a reflective expert. The educator has to know what information to share that the participants would find of most interest, how to share it in a way that is stimulating and keeps the participants' interest, and when to share just enough so they don't become overwhelmed by too much information.

This is where the second role of the nonformal educator comes into play, that of facilitator. This involves interacting with the learners in such a way that they feel more engaged in the experience. The facilitator has to balance the role of the expert. More specifically, this involves connecting personally with the learners, exploring their interests, creating opportunities for dialogue and exchange, and establishing a space for questions. It is also means being aware of how to share expertise discriminately, where it is most important and relevant, not just for the sake of showing how much the educator knows.

The facilitative approach is found among many nonformal educators, who spent time at the beginning of a tour or an interpretive hike getting to know the learners, establishing a rapport, and exploring the learners' reasons for attending the nonformal educational experience. A good example is Betty, a park naturalist, who believes it is fundamental to assess learners and explore ways to connect with their interests. Another example of facilitating is the emphasis on encouraging questions from the learners. Questions are often the primary means by which educator and learners engage each other. Both Phil, an interpretive guide, and Andrea, a docent, saw questions as essential to the nonformal experience. Other examples of a facilitative approach include the use of experiential activities through the promotion of hands-on activities, humor, and fun discussed in some detail in Chapter 4.

Through a reflective practice, educators can become more aware of these two roles and realize what role needs the most energy when leading an educational activity. It means asking yourself during a tour, for example, Am I being too much of an expert? How much am I allowing the learners to be involved, ask questions, and exchange ideas? Am I taking too much time interacting with the learners and not sharing with them what is important about the objects in the museum? Why am I spending more time on one role than the other? Is it a matter of comfort, confidence, or skill? Is it an institutional expectation? These questions help the educator use the roles more effectively based on the needs of the learners, the institutional expectations, and the contextual demands of the setting. Educators also become aware of their preferences and why; they have greater control over their practice; and they are able to more easily choose and shift their preferences in response to whatever demand emerges.

THE VISITOR AS A LEARNER

A second focus for the reflective educator is that of learning to see visitors who participate in a nonformal event as learners. Recognizing the visitors as learners is essential to developing an effective teaching practice that is responsive to their needs and interest. Seeing visitors as learners requires the educator to give attention to a variety of things that often would be overlooked if every participant were viewed as a visitor.

Thinking about visitors as learners requires the educator to regularly explore ways to teach that will improve and promote learning. An example is the non-reflective educator who was unaware of how the visitors in his tour were getting tired of standing and listening to him go on and on about a particular object in a museum. It was apparent that he was unaware of their concerns and was more interested in sharing his expertise. He wasn't thinking about his group of visitors as learners. If he had been, he would have more likely taken time through direct observation to reflect on how they were experiencing the tour. He might even have asked directly about how everyone was doing with the pace and process of the tour.

Thinking about visitors as learners prompts the educator to do several things in planning prior to the experience, as the event begins, and as it concludes. Most significantly, it provokes educators to look at the educational event through a learning lens, encouraging them to reflect on ways to design the event so it promotes learning. It means reflecting on questions, such as, What I have done in the past that seems to engage learners? What do I do at times that seems to discourage participation and interest? What are new ways that I can approach learners that will foster greater interest and participation?

As the event begins, thinking of visitors as learners reminds the educator to make a point to regularly assess the learners' individual interest and needs. Also, it helps to quickly establish a rapport and make connections early on in the event by demonstrating an interest in the learners and by engaging them on a personal level, if time allows. It helps to create a connection of being in sync emotionally with the learners and establishing a comfortable and supportive environment for learning. Also, it gives the educator the flexibility to modify the session in a timely manner in response to the unique interest of the learners. For example, in a tour of an old historic tavern, Mary was observed at the beginning of each tour asking if the learners were from the local area or from out of state. Based on this information, she provided greater or less background information about the geography and local history where the tavern was located.

Furthermore, thinking of visitors as learners reminds educators to recognize positionality such as race, class, gender, and age among learners and gauge the tour accordingly. In many tours of museums and historical sites, there are objects or events that have specific cultural significance to some learners more so than another. As in the formal setting, an effective educator takes the opportunity during an event to appreciate the differences that are reflected by the learners participating in the experience.

Furthermore, a reflective educator also spends time thinking about who is receiving the most attention on the tour. Am I am excluding some individuals? For example, when Rob led a tour of a historical museum of industry, most of the learners were men. The few women present rarely asked any questions. A response to this concern for educators would be to think of ways to engage the women more. The guides can make a particular point to spend time at certain aspects of the museum, such as historic pictures of women and children laborers. Another technique to draw quiet learners out is by asking them questions relevant to the tour.

As educators view visitors as learners it helps prompt them to continually assess the learners' state of mind throughout the educational experience. It means engaging in a heightened sense of "appraisal," continually assessing the learners' emotional states by observing eye contact, verbal interaction, and body language. It means noticing and at times asking whether learners are interested and engaged. If not, the response is to look for ways to foster curiosity, attention, and greater participation.

Finally, thinking of visitors as learners helps encourage educators to reflect on their teaching at the end of the event. This is the time to think about ways to improve their practice and be more responsive to the needs and interest of learners. Consequentially it is another way that helps balance the roles of expert and facilitator.

THE PUBLIC VERSUS PRIVATE CONTEXT

As discussed in Chapter 3, the nonformal context, or setting has a significant influence on practice. A wide range of contextual forces act on the educational experience, for example, distractions, learner heterogeneity, time constraints, novel setting and voluntary participation. The educator must give attention to these factors in concert with an awareness of a preferred approach to teaching. Without such preparation, the educator is at the mercy of the setting, like a ship without a rudder, with little chance to use the wind to advantage. Being aware of these forces, many which are unique to the nonformal setting, includes knowing how they interact with each other, and how they influence the educational experience.

One way to make sense of and respond to the factors that evolve from the nonformal context is through the use of two constructs that exist on a continuum: public versus private settings. Public means that the nonformal education setting is almost completely accessible to the public, most often by physical proximity, such as the self-help clinics located on a throughway in a home improvement store or an open tour of monuments in a historic battleground. It is not only accessible, but it is easy for participants to come and go as they please.

As we move away from more public settings toward more private settings, on the other end of the continuum, nonformal education is much less accessible. It has more barriers such as distance, entry fees, "off the main road," age requirements, and physical ability that the general public must overcome to enter the educational event. Participants generally arrive at these sites purposely, such as attending a museum tour or participating in a guided interpretive hike. These nonformal education programs might have admission criteria such as age or ability level. Once admitted, learners are led as a group and are often outside of public view. A good example of this is the tour of the artist's home mentioned in Chapter 4. It was located on a dirt road off a rural country byway. Organized visits were arranged in advance. Rarely did people stumble across this place and obtain access to the home. Also, all tours were guided. It could be argued that as the nonformal event becomes more private, it becomes more formal, potentially exhibiting some of the same characteristics found in more formal education.

So what does this continuum mean for the educator? It means a great deal. Where the nonformal setting falls along the continuum, the more the public or private the context will have a significant influence on practice. For example, the nonformal educators who were leading clinics in a public thoroughfare at a local home improvement store were teaching in a very different setting than the private tour in a historic home in the countryside. Also, it is important to note that even as a nonformal educational event unfolds it can shift back and forth between public and more private experiences. For example, I observed some museum tours that began in very public places and then became more private as the tour evolved, because the guide led the group into areas of the museum that were only accessible with a guide. Being aware of the setting, how it impacts practice, and how it might shift is essential if an educator is going to make the most of the nonformal setting. Understanding the differences in greater detail between these two settings is discussed below.

More Public Setting

A more public place easily accessible with almost no barriers is often in a place that can be observed by individuals involved in other activities. As a result, there are a number of factors that the educator needs to keep in mind. The first factor in more public settings is greater accessibility. The more accessible the nonformal experience, the more easily learners can enter and exit the event. This also means that others who choose not to participate directly are often able to observe and listen from the margins. A degree of this is found in some museum tours that are led in the midst of other visitors who are touring the museum on their own. Also, in these more public settings, the heterogeneity of the learners (age, level of interest) in the group is often quite varied, because access to the educational event is open, and there are no criteria for participation.

To understand the impact accessibility has on practice is to recognize its purpose in relationship to the nonformal experience, that of "attracting" learners to participate in the educational event. For example, as mentioned, many learners enter the home improvement clinics by happenstance, often pulled in by an interesting presentation. For some it is not something they originally planned to do, but instead they came upon it, and it piqued their interest. For example, at the tile-laying clinic, it was readily apparent that several learners were pulled into the event by the interesting presentation put on by the educator. For many it was not the original reason they came to the store. This explains to some extent why most nonformal educators spoke about making clinics fun.

The more public an event, the more the educator is pressured to become an "edutainer," performing before the learners and striving to be the center of attention. In these settings it is much more challenging to be a facilitator, allowing learners to play a role in directing the experience. Even though the educator knows how to be a facilitator in these settings, by quickly establishing a rapport with the learners, holding highly structured exchanges, and promoting well-orchestrated experiential activities that engage the learn-ers, the intent in a public event is not about promoting vistor-centeredness. Instead the goal is about maintaining their interest and keeping them from thinking about their feet as they stand and listen to the expert sharing information. There isn't much flexibility, despite its appearance, in what and how a clinic is taught or a tour is led.

Also, to put it bluntly, even though a clinic instructor may be an expert plumber, if the event can't attract and maintain the atten-tion of the learner, it is unlikely it will be perceived as a success. In more public settings, the success of the educational experience is apparent early on. The learners quickly dissipate if the educator can-not maintain their interest. A thoughtful educator in a more public setting would regularly assess the learners' level of interest, modify-ing the teaching approach accordingly, to ensure the best possible experience.

A second factor in more public settings is the number of dis-tractions, with many things competing for the learners' attention. This demands that the educator be acutely aware of the learners' interest and mood, and respond to them in a timely manner. If not, since this event is easily accessible, learners can be pulled away to some other interest, easily distracted, and exit as simply as they en-tered. In more public nonformal events, the "power of the feet" rests strongly with learners. This puts a good deal of pressure on the edu-cator to deliver and maintain interest. Furthermore, since the learn-ers can come and go with such ease, the level of expectation that educator has of the learner is generally low. There are few, if any, rules or requirements in order to participate in the educational event. Learners just show up, listen, and possibly, for a few, are given the opportunity to participate in an activity, such as practicing laying some tile. This low expectation shifts more responsibility from the learners to the educator to provide a successful educational experi-ence.

A third factor in more public nonformal events is the loosen-ing of social norms reflected in individual and group behavior. The more public the setting and the more freedom of access, the less participants seem bound by the norms such as paying attention and good visitor manners often associated with more private or formal educational experiences. It was not unusual to see individuals having side conversations, others not paying attention to the educator, and some being distracted by their children who did not have the patience to stand around and listen to a clinic about organizing closets. This can be a real teaching challenge.

Such teaching settings require the educator to be constantly aware of the learners' level of interest, working hard at providing an engaging experience, so participants stay focused. If their interest wanders or the competition for their attention is too great, the educator has little authority to pull them back in. This strategy is often just to move on, focus on the participants who are most engaged, and hope that the disinterested participants don't distract the others. This was most evident in the self-help clinics in the home improvement stores. The context of the store seemed to give individuals permission to engage in behaviors (side conversations, talking on cell phones) that would not be appropriate in more formal settings.

As the setting becomes more private, requiring more effort to participate, contextual factors and the interest of the learners begin to shift, all potentially influencing practice. Moving across the continuum to a midpoint between public and private nonformal education experiences, examples might include an open tour of historic monuments on a battlefield, a clinic held in a more private area of a store, or a campfire presentation on the geology of a state park. As events become less public and more private, the educator needs to develop an awareness of new influences on practice.

More Private Settings

The private nonformal education experience is more exclusive and held outside of public view. It requires greater purposefulness by learners in working through barriers, such as distance, time, cost, and admission criteria, in accessing the experience. Learners potentially take such an event more seriously, because they are more likely seeking these events. It is generally not something they just happened upon. Also, more control of the event seems to shift toward the educator and away from learners. In the more private setting the educator has greater influence on shaping the context and ultimately shaping the behavior of the participants.

To illustrate how things are different in more private settings, imagine yourself participating in the "moonwalk" at a local bird sanctuary late one cloudless summer evening. This moonwalk is a hike, led by Jim, an environmental educator, through the deep woods by the light of the moon. No flashlights are used and are only available in case of emergency. Through a guided moonwalk the learners had the opportunity to hear, if they were quiet, the busy life of nocturnal animals. This is an event that requires ground rules and asks for a high degree of commitment or engagement by the learners.

All the aspects of a more private educational experience are present in the moonwalk. It is a scheduled event that learners have to drive to at a time when most people are settling in for the evening. It is located in an isolated place and requires, for many individuals, an expert to participate. Also, for many adults, particularly individuals who grew up and live in urban environments, walking in the woods at night can be an unnerving experience, even more so without the constant use of a flashlight. In other words, in this and other more private educational experiences, expectations from the learners (safety, enjoyment) and from the educator (safety, following the rules) increase.

As the group gathered at the trailhead to begin the walk, Jim began by establishing a rapport, promoting confidence in his expertise and creating a comfortable learning environment. He ensured learners that this was a safe and fun experience if everyone followed directions. In this more private setting, Jim had a "captured" group of learners. It was more challenging for them to participate. Some had driven a good distance to the sanctuary and for some it was like an inconvenient time to be out. It would be even more challenging for them to leave, particularly once the activity was underway. Leaving the group in this setting would pose a great inconvenience to the entire group. Learners could not leave by themselves, because it was too great a risk at night. The guide would have to take the entire group back to the park entrance and possibly end the moonwalk for the evening if a learner wanted to withdraw after the walk had begun.

The issue of accessibility in a private setting as opposed to more public settings shifts more control of the experience and responsibility from the learners to the educator. This allows the educator to spend less energy focused on the learners' interests and more on the experience itself. Jim can assume from the beginning that, to some degree, the learners are highly interested because of the energy they have spent in getting to this experience.

This shift of control and the opportunity to work with a captured audience may seem on the surface a less challenging experience than teaching in more public settings. Yet it has its unique challenges as well. One of those challenges is the ease by which an educator can be drawn into complacency because of the difficulties learners face in leaving. As a result, it could be easy to overlook the need to be aware of the learners' interests. Furthermore, expectations from the learners increase in more private settings, so pressure increases for the educator to deliver an engaging experience that meets or exceeds the advance publicity. Learners have taken time and energy from their day to attend the event, and therefore, they want their "money's worth," making them potentially more critical.

So, in a more private setting the educator might have more latitude about choosing whether to act as a facilitator or an expert, because the learners have a high degree of interest. However, at the same time the expectations of the learners are generally much higher as well. Being aware of how the degree of public versus private context shapes an experience allows the educator to work in sync with these influences, respond accordingly, and shape the teaching to be responsive to the learners' needs.

INSTITUTIONAL EXPECTATIONS

The fourth focus for the reflective nonformal educator is institutional expectations. These are demands by the institution that oversees and governs the nonformal educational experience. It might be a museum board, the director of a local state park, or the central office of the home improvement store. It is whoever has the authority to establish the curriculum and other educational expectations, such as the time limit of interpretive hikes or the objects to be discussed. For some institutions, these expectations also include a particular educational philosophy or teaching approach. The more aware the reflective educator is of these expectations and from where they emanate, the more effective a working relationship with the institutions. Also, knowing who makes curriculum and program decisions allows the educator, the opportunity, if needed, to negotiate, program changes that are in the best interest of the learners.

These institutional expectations tend to fall within three areas: time, curriculum, and teaching approach. It is important to note that expectations most often originate locally in nonformal education programs as opposed to some larger national organization (Rogers, 2004). In the consumer self-help clinics, however, expectations emanated from the national offices of the different stores, often in the form of a script with lesson plans. For example, I observed most educators in the home improvement clinic having a clinic script at their side. However, as I previously pointed out, it was often not followed or referred to during the clinic itself.

The most evident institutional expectation is time constraints, as discussed in Chapter 3, where most of the experiences are short in duration and often take place with little opportunity to engage the learners. The period of time appropriated for the educational event, more than any other factor, influences how much the educator spends in the roles of expert and facilitator. The expert role is seen as much more expedient than the facilitative role, especially when there is a high level of interest by the institution in covering a lot of information. The facilitative role is much more time consuming, because of the opportunity to digress and be pulled off topic by learner questions. In response to the constant demands of time, a reflective educator has to be constantly aware of time limits and how much time is left. In the immediate term the question might be: How much time am I spending talking about a museum object? How long have we been observing and discussing this particular stone formation on an interpretive hike? How long have the learners been standing or sitting in one place? Through this increased awareness of time the educator is able to work within the time limits established by the institution and to be responsive to the attention span of the learners.

Another institutional expectation is the curriculum or the content of the education experience. Learning the curriculum is often one of the most challenging aspects for a nonformal educator, particularly for the naturalists and museum guides, where there is a great deal of information relevant to the setting. By knowing the curriculum they can provide a rich presentation and demonstrate a depth of understanding as they respond to an array of questions from learners. For example, in the tour of the artist's home, new docents are given a large notebook of information to become deeply familiar with. The notebook goes into great length about the artist, the home, and all the objects inside, including much more information than can ever be covered in a single tour. The docents spoke of spending many hours studying this notebook and observing other more experienced docents lead tours in preparation for leading a tour on their own.

To be able to make the most of the content, the educators needs to be aware of what the institution believes is important to share and what they consider most interesting. This involves creating a blend of both interests. Through an awareness of these varying and sometime competing interests, educators can share personal favorites, which will ultimately impact the overall quality of the experience.

Another issue to keep in mind is that the curriculum in any educational experience is never neutral or static; it is always changing and at times is contested (see Chapter 2). In other words, there are always different, sometimes divergent or competing stories within a museum, park, or clinic that could be shared with the learner. As discussed in Chapter 4, Eric, who taught about faux painting in a home improvement clinic, diverged from the script developed by the national office. He gave information that he found to be more accurate than what was provided by the home improvement store. To be aware of the various perspectives requires developing a deep expertise of the content. This should also remind educators that developing expertise requires staying current on the information about what they teach and being appreciative of different views, not just what is provided by the institution.

Also, it is important to pay attention to the questions that learners ask. At times they are going to disagree with the institution's interpretation of events. Educators must ask themselves if they are prepared to respond to the learners' queries. It is not always about having the "right" answer. It is also about, for example, developing an appreciation for different views about a historical event, how natural life should be appreciated, or possibly how a tool is used. The

Table 5.1 Reflective Questions to Help Nonformal Educators Teach with Their Eyes Wide Open

Expert versus Facilitator	Visitors as Learners	Public versus Private Context	Institutional Expectations
Which role am I spending the most time on? Am I being more of an expert or more of a facilitator? Why? How well am I connecting with the learners? How effectively am I sharing information? How much time am I spending talking to the learners? How much time am I listening and dialoguing with learners? Where is most of the learner's attention focused, on me or on the object or the novel setting?	Am I thinking about the visitors as learners? What is the learner's body language telling me? How are the learners feeling about the educational experience? What am I doing that is helping the learners remain engaged? What am I doing that might be discouraging learning? How I am making the most of the learner's positionality in relationship to the nonformal experience?	How public or private is this educational experience? How easy or difficult is it for learners to enter and leave? What distractions are around that might draw the learner's attention away? What can I do help the learners not think about leaving? What is it about the setting that I can use to my advantage to make the learners more engaged?	What content does my institution expect me to cover during the nonformal experience? What about the content do I find most interesting and enjoyable to share? How well am I making the most of the time available? How much am I allowing the learner time to discuss and reflect on the content? How open am I to differing perspectives about the story being told?

engagement of multiple perspectives can at times offer a more en-riching and engaging learning experience. Furthermore, challeng-ing questions should prompt educators to explore on a regular basis what new information is available about the topic. Staying current helps educators be more aware of the competing perspectives that surround the topic, and it also helps keep their own passion and interest alive and growing as they engage in teaching in nonformal settings. Table 5.1 offers a quick reference to a set of reflective questions relevant to the four key aspects of the nonformal practice.

CONCLUSION

This chapter will help nonformal educators develop a reflective practice in which they become aware of how their teaching approach impacts learners' experiences in concert with the nonformal setting. Educators can't focus on just one role (expert versus facilitator), as they have to keep all of the factors in mind when making decisions about teaching. The set of questions in Table 5 are designed to help educators teach with their eyes wide open, focusing on the four key areas of the nonformal practice:

1. There two primary roles (expert and facilitator).
2. The visitors as learners.
3. The context as public and private space.
4. The institutional expectations.

Thoughtful answers lead to greater self-awareness and therefore more effective teaching as the educational experience unfolds.

CHAPTER 6

Coming Full Circle

As we near the end of the book, it is important to return the discussion about nonformal education back to the academic literature. What have we learned from these case studies that changes the way we might think about nonformal education in relationship to other types of education (formal, participatory) and learning (informal, incidental)? To set the context for this discussion, it is necessary to review some of the major concerns that exist with the present way nonformal education is presented in the literature.

CONCERNS WITH TRADITIONAL ASSUMPTIONS

One concern is that the name "nonformal" itself is problematic. Nonformal implies "not" formal, creating a binary relationship, such that everything that is formal education, nonformal is not. It is plain to see now that this is not the case. In fact, there are many shared characteristics between both types of education. For example, as the case studies illustrate, on the surface, nonformal education may seem somewhat learner-centered, flexible, and with few outside influences, but in reality it is equally if not more often teacher-centered, structured, with an emphasis on sharing information within significant time constraints, institutional expectations, and an ever shifting context. Many of the same teaching methods found in more formal settings such as a transmission approach and questioning are quite prevalent in nonformal settings. Also, an inherent trait to both types is that an educator is present, although the role may be different at times in relationship to the learner.

Two, this traditional binary comparison (nonformal versus formal) oversimplifies the complexity that exists within and across these different types of education. It can lead to a lack of appreciation for the challenges nonformal educators face when going about their work. This is particularly evident when reviewing Table 2.1 in Chapter 2, which presents practices of teaching, many of which are anecdotally derived and substantiated. Furthermore, it overlooks the multifaceted and contextually responsive approach required to teach in nonformal settings.

Models of nonformal education have become more complex (e.g., Brennan, 1997), where efforts have been made in developing frameworks for understanding the various types of nonformal education (e.g., Rogers, 2005) to illustrate its relationship to other forms of education. Yet, there still is an over-reliance on simplistic assumptions about the nature of teaching within these settings. In other words, the identification of these types seems to imply, with little critique or research, that there is an inherent approach to teaching formally and another approach to nonformal teaching. For example in Rogers (2005) continuum model, it implies that the more local the education, the more flexible the curriculum and, therefore, the more responsive this education is to the needs of the participants. This form of logic continues with the idea that since nonformal education is supposedly more responsive, then the teaching approach must be "learner-centered." This is not to say that these kinds of assumptions don't ever manifest in practice, but as revealed from these case studies, teaching in nonformal settings is generally not indicative of this assumed singular learner-centered approach. Furthermore, it seems to imply that this is the way that teaching needs to or should take place in nonformal education.

The implications of this rudimentary logic and implicit educational agenda that frame the discussion in the literature about nonformal education are significant. They not only present an inaccurate picture of what is actually going on in these settings, but they may also indirectly establish a set of expectations or standards by which educators judge themselves or are judged by others when evaluating the practice of teaching in nonformal settings.

Despite these concerns, however, the concept of nonformal education, crude in its conception, is very important to the field of adult education and education in general. As Rogers (2004) and Brennan (1997) argue, naming it gives this ubiquitous type of education credibility as a viable educational endeavor. And it gives a voice to a host of educators, often unheard and unappreciated, about the educational contributions they are making in the world every day. Nonformal education also offers a place for a disparate and diverse group of educational programs that fall outside of formal institutions and provides a place to come together and learn from other's successes and failures, instead of operating in isolation. The question now is where do we go from here? What have we learned from these case studies that contributes to a better framework for understanding teaching in nonformal education in relationship to itself and to formal education?

REVISING TWO PERSPECTIVES

When this book was initially conceptualized it seemed that a likely byproduct would be the development of a new framework for thinking about nonformal education in relationship to other types or forms of education. However, after much reflection it became apparent that this was a bit ambitious, since the focus was about how to make meaning of teaching within nonformal settings, and much less about nonformal education as educational system, its varying purposes, and how it relates to other types of education. Also, despite the critique of Brennan's and Roger's frameworks of nonformal education, these models have accomplished, to some degree, what they had set out to do. With some additional modifications, they could be even more effective at contributing to an understanding of nonformal education in developed countries.

The first and most sweeping modification is that the nature of teaching in nonformal settings cannot be described as a singular instructional approach. It cannot be defined by the goals or objectives of a program, from a location of a program in relationship to its participants, or from the relationship of a program to a more formal educational system. Teaching in nonformal settings, or in any other setting, involves too many variables to predict what instructional approach is to be implemented or should be implemented by a program. This means moving away from a modern, grand narrative perspective of nonformal education to a more postmodern, multiple narrative and situated view. This view appreciates a variety of instructional approaches in response to a collection of competing factors present in nonformal settings. Those factors, discussed in Chapter 5, include the roles of the educator, the visitor as learner, public versus private settings, and institutional expectations. All need to be considered by educators when making decisions about teaching in nonformal settings. This view also means recognizing the educator is both being shaped by these factors and is shaping these factors as the experience unfolds. The challenge for scholars and practitioners of nonformal education is continually developing a better understanding of these and other factors when making decisions about teaching.

Despite this strong caveat, these case studies do provide some insight into how to better understand what nonformal education is, and what it is in relationship to more formal education. By better edifying this relationship, it reminds educators what they need to consider in a particular setting. It also has implications for program developers and policy makers when designing for delivery of particular content or responding to the educational demands of a particular group.

To bring to life a richer understanding of nonformal education it is best to build or draw upon previous work (Rogers 2005; Brennan 1997) in relationship to what has been learned in the case studies.

Along a Continuum

To understand nonformal education in relationship to formal education, as Rogers (2004, 2005) has done, is to think about these two constructs along a continuum (see Figure 6.1). Each type of education would be at opposite ends, and the space in between would reflect gradations of each type of education. No other types of education or learning, such as participatory education and informal learning are included, as participatory education implies a particular educational in teaching rather than a type of education. Likewise, informal learning is about learning, not about a type of education; and it is a form of learning that exists in all educational settings.

However, the continuum is the only similarity to Roger's model. His model is rooted in the idea that nonformal education is more responsive to local interests and needs. It is as if the individual's or

Figure 6.1 A continuum of education (Rogers, 2004).

local community's interests are the impetus for the nonformal educational experience, and that those interests imply a need for a particular educational approach. The actual setting or place of this educational program is less relevant, as long as it is located near the learners. On the other hand, in the case studies the setting is paramount and central. Often the very location of the learning is what draws the learners into the nonformal experience. For example, without a natural state park, there wouldn't be a bird walk. Without a museum, there wouldn't be a tour of artifacts and rare objects. In these case studies and in many similar nonformal sites, the setting is essential to the educational experience. The setting is so central, that if it is not of interest to learners, they most likely will not attend. Furthermore, often an educator cannot easily transfer the curriculum located in one setting to just any other setting. For many, the curriculum is situated within the setting.

Keeping that thought in mind, the overarching factor that determines where a program falls on the continuum (see Figure 6.2) is the public accessibility of the educational setting. As discussed in Chapter 5, the more a program becomes available and accessible to the general public, the more it reflects nonformal education; and the less public and less accessible it is, the more it moves toward formal education. For example, the self-help clinics exemplify nonformal education. They are located in a very public setting and are easily accessible by learners. Little is present to act as barriers to voluntary participation, disregarding the need of transportation to get to the

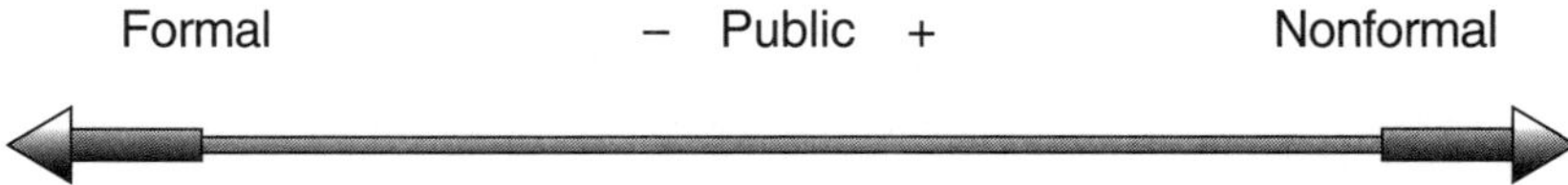

Figure 6.2 A continuum of education in public places.

store. There are no restrictions on who can attend and no rules or guidelines that have to be followed or met by learners beyond everyday social norms expected within public settings.

Other very public nonformal education programs include a health mobile setup at a state fair to check and educate the public about the importance of regularly measuring blood pressure and cholesterol levels; or a roadside clinic set up at a highway rest stop to educate parents about the proper use of child restraint seats and provide a venue for educating drivers about safety tips such as tire pressure, safety belts, and taking breaks when driving during the holidays. This kind of nonformal programming generally takes place in very public settings where there is easy access to a great cross-section of the populace. Also, the setting, particularly the roadside clinic, is specifically relevant to the educational experience. These more public forms of nonformal education are both a way to have an immediate impact on an individual's life and an opportunity to further educate people on broader social issues.

Along with the degree of how public a program is are several other contextual factors, such as time constraints, heterogeneity of learners, novel setting, and voluntary participation, that shed further light on this continuum. As an educational program moves toward the nonformal end, these factors are generally heightened, or there is a greater likelihood for them to be present (see Figure 6.3). The figure illustrates this by a "+" sign. For example, returning to the home improvement clinic, the opportunity to engage learners more than once is unlikely, and time is very limited for the educational experience. Second, since this nonformal experience has a greater degree of public access, meaning that learners can enter and

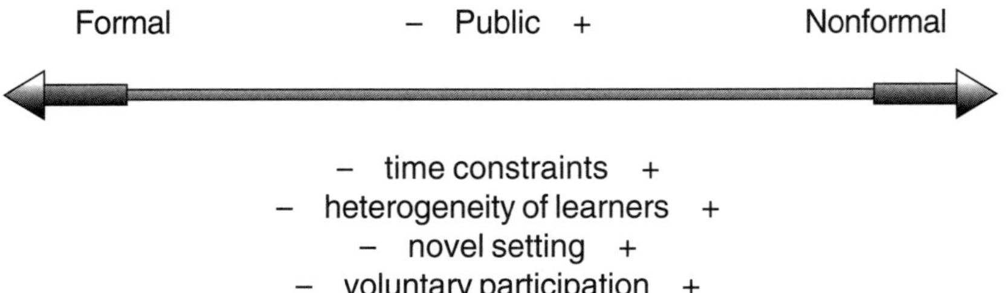

Figure 6.3 A continuum of education in public places.

leave easily, it is likely there will be high degree of heterogeneity (wide range of learners in understanding of the clinic topic, age, gender, race, and so on). Third, due to this greater heterogeneity and the potential time limitations, it is more challenging to develop relationships and a sense of community among learners. Fourth, the novel setting, the location of the nonformal educational program, is significant to the clinics' success, both in attracting learners and making the learning experience more authentic. Potentially, the educator can become less central, since the setting plays a significant role in the experience. Fifth, voluntary participation, or free choice, is very high in this setting, with learners coming and going easily with few constraints, as the educational experience unfolds.

On the other end of the continuum where formal education is found, the setting is less accessible to the public, in essence it is much more private (noted by the "-" symbol). More private, less public access means that there are generally more physical and mental barriers for learners to overcome to access the educational programming. More formal programs often require payment and there are at times criteria such as age, test scores, and prior educational credentials required of learners, before they can participate in the experience. As the education becomes more private and formal, it generally requires greater commitment by learners as to what is required to complete the educational experience. This also often involves a commitment to travel geographically. In other words, it is unlikely that a learner would walk into or stumble upon a private, formal educational experience. Furthermore, often the program is not located where the general public can easily access it. In others words, the more formal programs are located in a less than public place, in a building designated for them which has to be entered purposefully by the learner.

At the same time, many of the factors that shed light on nonformal educational programming are starting to change considerably. For example, in an adult high school evening program located in a downtown high school building, its geographical location, possibly one classroom, is quite removed from the general public, thus making it more formal. Its location alone implies a more private, less inclusive form of education. When looking at the other factors listed in Figure 6.3, there are other changes as well. Time constraints in the more private, formal setting are not as limiting, as the likelihood of seeing learners multiple times is much greater, and classes are repeated generally over a longer period of time. Similarly, learner heterogeneity has lessened considerably, particularly their educational backgrounds, because a more formal education program attracts similar learners. In the case of the adult high school evening program, these are learners who have similar educational backgrounds and interest in completing their high school diplomas. Also, due to the opportunity of repetitive engagement by learners and due to their similar interests, there is a greater likelihood for relationship building and community to develop among learners and educators, which clearly differs from a once-and-done clinic.

Concerning the novel setting, the adult high school classroom is not novel and not very authentic, and as discussed earlier, the setting is significant only due to its geographical location. It is close to those who need it. Furthermore, the content of the program could most likely be taught anywhere and in any classroom, and the setting is generally not as relevant to the learning experience. Also, since the setting is not novel, the educator is likely to be more central to the educational experience, both in content and direction. Although, this is a guarded observation, because the educator could choose an approach is more learner-centered despite the setting. Lastly, voluntary participation, although present, is restricted to those who need a high school degree. The educators would most likely turn away learners who were over or under-qualified, so as not to take a seat from those most in need.

So what does this new continuum mean for other educational programs often considered to be nonformal? Consider an adult literacy program located in a community center in rural Pennsylvania or a Farmer Field School (community-based agriculture development program) located in western Kenya. Without going through all the related contextual factors, this analysis focuses predominantly on the novel setting and time constraints. The literacy program could most likely be taught anywhere in that community, although it is best taught where it is easily accessible by those who need it. However, the setting itself most likely has little relevancy to the teaching and learning experience. In other words, the curriculum could be transferred to any geographical location if need be. Also, time constraints are not as limited, due to multiple classroom opportunities to engage learners. Therefore, a literacy program based on this model would be closer to the formal education end of the continuum.

Similarly, the Farmer Field Schools are geographically situated within a community by farm fields where the participants can experiment with different crops, soil conditions, types of fertilizers, and so forth. The setting in this situation is much more novel and authentic than in the literacy program, and, therefore, more significant to the teaching and learning experience. Also, although possible, it would be more difficult to offer this program, or this curriculum, in another setting. Based on this analysis, the Farmer Field Schools are closer to the nonformal end of the continuum, but not as far as some other nonformal programs. Like the literacy program, time constraints are minimized because of multiple opportunities for the educator to engage learners and develop longer-term relationships.

There are even programs that seem to be in the middle of the continuum, like the moonwalk at night in the bird sanctuary. This educational experience is located in an isolated place, is more challenging to access, and is restricted to those who are physically and mentally capable of walking in the woods at night. This places it more toward the formal end of the continuum. At the same time, the setting is unique and central to the experience. Also, the opportunity to engage the audience repetitively is limited, moving the experience toward nonformal education, somewhere in the middle of the continuum.

What is important in this new model is not so much labeling a particular program formal or nonformal. The goal is to develop a greater appreciation for other factors, not previously considered, that play a significant role in shaping practice. The model should remind the reader of how these factors change as the educational setting shifts. Furthermore, despite the effort in giving greater clarity to the two types of education along a continuum (more formal or nonformal), it is important to note that little effort was made to draw any conclusions about the teaching approach within and between these particular settings. This can't be stressed enough. As discussed in Chapter 5, in deciding the most appropriate teaching approach, educators have to consider the contextual factors of the setting (public versus private). They also need to consider how they perceive their role as expert versus facilitator, the learner versus visitor, and the institutional expectations.

This new continuum provides a way to make sense of nonformal education in relationship to more formal education along a continuum of private and public settings and in relationship to factors that shape practice. The next section is an effort to provide a better understanding of the different types of nonformal education, defined by their objectives.

An Integrative Perspective

The continuum in Figure 6.3 provides a way to think about nonformal education in relationship to formal education. Now it is time to think about nonformal education in relationship to itself. This section will build on Brennan's (1997) model, discussed in Chapter 2, and continue with the same name, an integrative perspective. It is important to rethink this model so it is more representative of nonformal education in developed countries and recognizes nonformal efforts located in cultural institutions such as museums, parks, zoos, and libraries. As previously discussed, these institutions are so prevalent in North America that they easily exceed the number of more formal adult education institutions such as adult high schools, adult basic education programs, and higher education institutions.

In response to the lack of representation of cultural institutions in Brennan's model (complementing, alternative, supplementing), adding a fourth type of nonformal education seems appropriate: heritage education. Heritage education is found in cultural institutions that were created to "preserve history that is passed on to future generations and to provide public places for learning and recreation" (Taylor, Parrish, & Banz, 2010). Museums, libraries, zoos, and parks all share the primary purpose of providing public places to preserve communities' cultural heritages represented by the objects, specimens, and sites the communities most value. These are places for learning and recreation and offer educational resources for both formal education and lifelong learning.

In addition, based on the review of the related literature on nonformal education and the case studies, several additional revisions to Brennan's model will make it more representative of nonformal education in Western countries. The first revision involves broadening the meaning of *complementing* education to include education that not only focuses on basic adult education, but also includes forms of education that complement formal education, such as health and safety education. For example, the University of Iowa has a mobile clinic that offers free health screening and education to underserved populations in and around Iowa City, Iowa (The University of Iowa Mobile Clinic, 2009). Another example is the "Free Learn-to-Row" Clinics offered by the Hudson River Rowing Association in Poughkeepsie, New York (Hudson River Rowing Association, 2009). These programs often are highly instrumental and skills-based nonformal educational programming.

The second revision involves broadening the meaning of *alternative* nonformal education to include not only indigenous/tribal education, but also nonformal education programs that recognize and promote diverse lifestyles and ways to relate to the world differently from mainstream society. Examples include in more developed countries intentional community education (e.g., Intentional Communities), and nonformal environmental/sustainability education (e.g., Project Wild, Community Works) to mention a few.

A similar revision is suggested for the *supplemental* type of nonformal education, which for developing countries focuses on education for promoting democracy and capitalism (Brennan, 1997). In Western countries, which are predominantly democratic, this type would be revised to include education that helps citizens in fostering a democratic society, for example, the National Issues Forum. I would also include programs that assist learners such as immigrants and refugees to be effective members of this society. For example, the International Institute of Minnesota offers citizenship services that include classes to help learners prepare for their citizenship exam. The supplemental type of nonformal education also includes programming that promotes advocacy education, educating historically marginalized groups (class, race, gender) about their rights as citizens and workers (Consumer Rights Education, 2009; Lambda Legal, 2009). Two good examples are the VOZ Worker's Rights Edu-

Table 6.1 Revision of Brennan's Model of Types of Nonformal Education

Complementing	Alternative	Supplemental	Heritage
Adult literacy Programs	Indigenous education	Political education	Museums
			Zoos
GED program	Tribal schools	Citizenship education	National parks
English as a secnd language	Intentional community education	Consumer advocacy	Libraries
Health and safety education	Sustainability education	Worker's rights education	
Consumer education			

cation Project, a nonformal program that provides publications, cultural events, and educational workshops to help secure and protect worker's rights in the northwest United States (Matta, 2006); and Lamda Legal (2009), that advocates for gay rights and recently offered a nonformal education program titled: "Take the power: A life and estate planning symposium." These revisions to Brennan's model are summarized in Table 6.1.

It is important to recognize that this framework has many of the same challenges that were discussed in Chapter 2 about Brennan's original model. The program examples above often overlap into other categories. There are libraries that play a significant role in complementing the present formal educational system and at the same time, they are sites for nonformal citizenship education. Likewise, it could be argued that some museums and historical sites reflect supplemental nonformal education, because they are educating citizens about the accomplishments and benefits of a democratic society, such as the United States. Regardless, this framework is an effort to bring attention to the vast array of nonformal educational programming that exists in any country. Through this recognition further work can be done to better understand the educational contributions of these nonformal programs.

IMPLICATIONS FOR NONFORMAL
PROGRAM DEVELOPMENT

What is the point? Why go to all this trouble of more accurately identifying nonformal education programs? Why discuss both the different types of nonformal programs and their relationship to formal programs, if it isn't possible to draw a definitive conclusion about a teaching approach in these settings? In response to these questions, it is important to reiterate that this model does have implications for teaching. It reminds educators that there isn't one particular approach to teaching in any setting. It also begins to shed light on factors to consider when making decisions about what teaching approach to take, regardless of setting. Also, beyond teaching, this model can assist individuals who are involved in developing educational nonformal programs.

Like teaching, being aware of the revised models helps program developers make more informed decisions when planning new nonformal programs. If, for instance, program developers are considering the design of an easily accessible nonformal program in a more public setting, what are some factors they need to consider to help ensure a successful learning experience? What are the unique challenges they will face, educationally, working within a very public arena? Also, what other nonformal programs sharing similar goals and objectives could offer some insight? In answering these question and others it is best to discuss them in context to a real educational challenge going on in the world today.

For example, take the present economic crisis with high mortgage foreclosures, loss of jobs, poor credit, and so forth. People have a real need for financial literacy programs to help them gain confidence and control of their personal finances. Despite this need, it can be very difficult for people to enter a government office and participate in educational programming, particularly about a topic so personal. In response, program planners could explore the array of nonformal programming available by using Brennan's revised integrative perspective discussed in the previous section. After this review a possible response to consider is *complementing* nonformal education. This could be a means of helping learners in need of financial literacy education, since it builds on skills and knowledge found in the more formal school settings. Similar complementing programs could be reviewed, for instance, literacy and adult basic education programs, to compare the shared challenges, potential successes, and best practices.

As program developers decide on the type of nonformal education, they can also consider the optimum setting, whether public versus private, for the financial literacy program. An initial approach is using Roger's revised continuum to develop an understanding of the broad factors that play out in various nonformal settings. For example, consider what is involved if they choose to place the financial literacy program in a more public setting.

The benefits of locating the financial literacy program in a high traffic area, like a self-help clinic in a home retail store, near an unemployment office, could pique the interest of potential learners. The clinic could provide material for learners to take home and read further on their own. It can also offer a venue to collect contact information for follow-up for those interested in receiving assistance in a more private setting. With the right approach, promoting high novelty, such as easily noticeable signage, possibly some individual reward such as food, drink for attending, the educational program might make a significant impact similar to the mobile health clinic at a street festival or auto safety programs at highway rest areas.

On the other hand the program developers need to be aware of the inherent challenges of a more public nonformal setting. For one, in settings where it is easy for learners to enter the educational event, it will be just as easy for them to leave. Another challenge is the greater likelihood of distractions associated with more public settings. The programmers need to think about ways to maintain their learners' interest and likewise provide a program of short duration. This means that only the most pertinent financial literacy information could be shared. Also, the easier the access, the greater the likelihood there will be participants whom the program cannot serve. In other words, the program would have to be designed so that it is timely and responsive, so people can easily decide on their own if the program is relevant to their individual needs.

Continuing with this example, consider the possibility that after much discussion and planning, the program developers realize that even though the nonformal financial literacy program may pique the interest of the learners and share pertinent information, there is just too much relevant material to cover in such a brief venture. A response to this concern would be moving along the continuum toward more private nonformal programming.

More private programming would be less public, such as locating the financial literacy program in a small classroom available in the unemployment office. The benefits are that the educator will have the time to cover the necessary information and address individual needs. The setting has fewer distractions and is likely a more comfortable learning experience. However, as in any educational venture, there are still challenges. A more formal setting will likely have a lower number of learners, because of greater demands, motivation (commitment to complete the program), time constraints (scheduling), and other barriers (transportation, cost).

One other approach to this program on financial literacy is a merging of the types of nonformal education. The more public approach can complement and assist the more private program at the same location. The more public approach serves to both attract and screen those who need further assistance, which they can readily receive in the more private nonformal programming in the same location. In other words, after a brief session, those learners who want additional help can attend a more private program.

For program developers, becoming aware of these types of nonformal education and recognizing the related contextual factors are beneficial. It both broadens the educational opportunities for engaging learners and increases the likelihood of successful programming. It can also remind program developers that these types of education should not be seen in opposition to each other. They are on a continuum, each type reflecting aspects of the other, potentially providing ways to complement and build on each other's strengths and minimize each other's challenges.

FUTURE STUDY OF NONFORMAL EDUCATION

By this time the reader has a better understanding of the complex nature of teaching in nonformal education settings. Possibly there are even some who are actively engaged or are considering teaching in such settings. The goal has been to guide them in reflecting about their approach to teaching, how they think about learners, how public versus private settings affect the experience, and what institutional expectations are associated with their programs. Other educators may now be more aware of how their nonformal programs are similar and different from other nonformal programs, leading to greater understanding of how to improve their own approaches to nonformal education. If the latter has been accomplished, then many of the objectives of this book have been met.

Now, where does the study of nonformal education go from here? What new directions should be taken in the areas of research and practice? Before exploring these broad questions, it is important to note that this work only scratches the surface of what is known about teaching in nonformal settings. In response to this concern and in an effort to address the questions above, three areas have been identified that would extend the work that has been started here regarding the relationship of nonformal education to formal education and the different types of nonformal education in existence.

First, what is missing from the models discussed in this book is the learners' perspective. At present, these models are derived from observations of learners and a mining of the educators' perspectives of teaching in nonformal settings. More descriptive research is needed on how learners make meaning of the nonformal setting. What do they see as influencing their decision of when to participate in or when to leave a nonformal educational event? What do the learners feel is most important when it comes to learning in a nonformal setting? What instructional approaches do they find most helpful? Also, what is their perception of private versus public settings in how it influences their level of participation, interest, and overall assessment of the experience? Adding the visitors' perspective to what has already been observed would provide a richer understanding of the nonformal experience.

Second, there needs to be work on many other nonformal educational settings beyond those investigated in this book. Reflecting on Brennan's model, it means making a similar effort to identify types of nonformal programs that were not included here, such as supplemental and alternative types of nonformal education. This would involve looking at more indigenous and lifestyle education, as well as citizen and advocacy education.

Looking at additional programs can provide the opportunity to more fully substantiate the integrity of the revised version of Brennan's model, as well as factors that inform the continuum relationship between formal and nonformal education. It is likely that there are other factors in addition to the ones identified that have significant influence on practice:

- public versus private
- time constraints
- heterogenity of learners
- novel setting
- voluntary participation

Third, building on the latter point, there is also a need for a different approach to researching nonformal education. Now that a framework for identifying these programs has been developed, it provides the opportunity to do a large-scale study, or survey, involving both nonformal educators and learners across many programs, inclusive of all types. This research agenda would more fully substantiate the assumptions made in this book and, at the same time, provide a resource for nonformal programs across the country.

CONCLUSION

Much has been learned about nonformal education. Probably most significant is the varied nature of teaching regardless of the type of education (formal, nonformal). Teaching in nonformal settings is not predetermined, but ever shifting, based on a variety of contextual factors. Developing an awareness of these factors leads to a richer understanding about the differences between formal and nonformal education. Furthermore, exploring teaching in museums, parks, and consumer education sites has resulted in giving attention to education in cultural institutions, a type of nonformal education often overlooked. It has also provided greater clarity to other types and settings, particularly in developed countries. Through this new understanding, educators and program developers are more informed about how to instruct and develop nonformal education programs.

REFERENCES

Ahmed, M., & Coombs, P. H. (Eds). (1975). *Education for rural development.* New York: Praeger.

Beckerman, Z., Burbules, N. C., & Silberman-Keller, D. (2006). Introduction. In Z. Beckerman, N. C. Burbles, & D. Silberman-Keller (Eds.). *Le arning in places* (pp. 1-8), New York: Peter Lang.

Beckman, E. A. (1999). Evaluating visitors' reactions to interpretation in Australian national parks. *Journal of Interpretation Research, 4*(1), 5-19.

Bitgood, S. (2002). Environmental psychology of museums, zoos, and other exhibition centers. In R. Bechtel & A. Churchman (Eds.) *Handbook of environmental psychology* (pp. 461-480). San Francisco: John Wiley & Sons.

Bock, J. C., & Bock, C. M. (1989). Nonformal education policy: Developing countries. In C. J. Titmus (Ed.), *Lifelong education for adults: An international handbook* (pp. 64-69), Oxford: Pergamon Press.

Bock, J. C., & Papagiannis, G. J. (1983). Some alternative perspectives on the role of nonformal education in national development. In J. C. Bock & G. J. Papagiannis (Eds.). *Nonformal education and national development* (pp. 3-21). New York: Praeger.

Borg, C., Cauchi, B., & Mayo, P. (2006). Museum education as cultural contestation. In C. Borg & P. Mayo (Eds.). *Learning and social difference* (pp. 75-89). London: Paradigm.

Brembeck, C. (1973). *Nonformal education as an alternative to schooling .* East Lansing, MI: Michigan State University.

Brennan, B. (1997). Reconceptualizing non-formal education. *International Journal of Lifelong Education, 16*(3), 185-200.

Brody, M., & Tomkiewicz, W. (2002). Park visitors' understandings, values and beliefs related to their experience at Midway Geyser Basin, Yellowstone National Park, USA. *International Journal of Science Education, 24*(11), 1119-41.

Busque, L. (1991) Potential interaction and potential investigation of science center exhibits and visitors interest. *Journal of Research in Science Teaching, 28*, 411-421, 1991.

Cabral, M. (2005). Democratisation and access to cultural heritage in Brazil. In J. Thinesse-Demel (Ed.). *Museums, libraries, and cultural heritage* . Report on the workshop held at CONFINTEA V Mid-term Review Conference, Bangkok, Thailand: UNESCO.

Carr, D. (1991). Living on one's own horizon: Cultural institutions, school libraries, and lifelong learning. *School Library Media Quarterly, 19*(4), 217-222.

Chadwick, A., & Stannett, A. (Eds.). (2000). *Museums and the education of adults.* Leicester, UK: NIACE.

Colonial Williamsburg. (2008). *Great Hopes Plantation.* Retrieved April 30, 2009, from http://www.history.org/Almanack/places/hb/hbgrthopes.cfm

Community Works. (2009).On-line resource center . Retrieved June 19, 2009, from http://www.vermontcommunityworks.org/cwabout/index.htm

Consumer Rights Education. (2009). *Consumer recovery network.* Retrieved on June 17, 2009 from http://www.consumerrecoverynetwork.com/consumer_rights.html

Coombs, P. H. (1968). *The world educational crisis: A system analysis.* New York: Oxford University Press.

Coombs, P. H. (1975). Nonformal education: Myths, realities, and opportunities. *Comparative Education Review, 20*(3), 281-293.

Coombs, P. H., & Ahmed, M. (1974). *Attacking rural poverty: How nonformal education can help.* London: John Hopkins University Press.

Courtenay, S. (1991). Defining adult and continuing education. In S. B. Merriam & P. M. Cunningham (Eds.), *Handbook of adult and continuing education* (pp. 15-25). San Francisco: Jossey-Bass.

Daloz, L. P., Daloz, S., Keen, C. H., & Keen, J. P. (1996). *Common fire: Lives of commitment in a complex world.* Boston: Beacon Press.

Dave, R. H. (1973). *Lifelong education and the school.* UIE Monograph No. 1. Hamburg: UNESCO Institute for Education.

Davidson, P., & Black, R. (2007). Voices from the profession: Principles of successful guided cave interpretation. *Journal of Interpretation Research, 12*(2), 25-43.

Demas, S., & Scherer J. A. (2002, April). Esprit de Place: maintaining and designing library buildings to provide transcendent spaces. *American Libraries*, 65-68.

Dudzinska-Przesmitzki, D., & Grenier, R. (2008). *Nonformal and informal adult learning in museums: A literature review. 33*(1), 9-22.

Evans, D. R. (1981). *The planning of nonformal education.* Paris: United Nations Educational, Scientific and Cultural Organization.

Ewert, D. M. (1989). Adult education and international development. In S. B. Merriam & P. M. Cunningham (Eds.), *Handbook of adult and continuing education* (pp. 84-98). San Francisco: Jossey-Bass.

Eysenck, M. W., & Calco, M. G. (1992). Anxiety and performance: The processing efficiency theory. *Cognition and Emotions, 6,* 409-434.

Falk, J. H. (Ed.). (2001). *Free-choice science education.* New York: Teacher's College Press.

Falk, J. H. (2004). *The director's cut: Toward an improved understanding of learning from museums.* Institute for Learning Innovation, Office of Director, 166 West Street, Annapolis, MD 21401. Online in Wiley InterScience http://www.interscience.wiley.com

Falk, J. H., & Dierking, L. D. (2002) *Lessons without limits.* New York: Rowman and Littlefield.

Falk, J. H., Koran, J. J., Jr., & Dierking, L. D. (1986). The things of science: Assessing the learning potential of science museums. *Science Education, 70,* 503-508.

Harmon, D. (1976). Recurrent and nonformal education: A definitional prelude. In D. Harman (Ed.) *Expanding recurrent and nonformal education.* New Directions in Higher Education, No. 14 (pp. 1-6). San Francisco: Jossey-Bass.

Harris, C. (2007). Libraries with lattes: The new third place. *Aplis 20*(4), 145-152.

Heimlich, J. E. (1993). *Nonformal environmental education: Toward a working definition.* Columbus, OH: Educational Resources Information Center. (ERIC Document Reproduction Service No. ED360154).

Hitch, J., & Youatt, J. P. (2002). *Communicating family and consumer sciences: A guidebook for professionals.* Tinley Park, IL: Goodheart-Willcox.

Hooper-Greenfield, E. (2000). *Museums and the interpretation of visual culture.* London: Routledge.

Hudson River Rowing Association. (2009). Coaching and safety clinics. Retrieved June 14, 2009, from http://www.hudsonriverrowing.org/Programs/Clinics.htm

Intellectual Freedom Basics. (2008). Intellectual Freedom and Censorship Q & A. Retrieved July 4, 2008, from http://www.ala.org/ala/aboutala/offices/oif/basics/intellectual.cfm, P 3.

Intentional Communities (2009). *Fellowship for intentional communities.* Retrieved May 17, 2009, from http://www.ic.org/

International Institute of Minnesota. (2009). *Serving people in transition.* Retrieved June 15, 2009, from http://www.iimn.org/

Jarvis, P. (1987). *Adult learning in a social context.* London: Croom Helm.

Lambda Legal. (2009). *Take the power: A life and estate planning symposium.* Retrieved on June 17, 2009, from http://www.lambdalegal.org/take-action/events/take-the-power-a-life-and-5.html

Livingstone, D. W. (2006). Informal learning: Conceptual distinctions and preliminary findings. In N. C. Burbules & D. Silberman-Keller (Eds.). *Learning in places* (pp. 203-228). New York: Peter Lang.

Manikowske, L., Stone, J., Farr, B., Wilson, J., & Wintersteen, W. (2002). Teaching about chemical resistant gloves with educational exhibits. *Journal of Family and Consumer Sciences, 94(*4), 34-40.

Marsick, V. J., & Watkins, K. E. (1990). *Informal and incidental learning in the workplace.* London: Routledge.

Matta, C. (2006). VOZ Workers' rights education project. *Justice Journal: News and Events from the Progressive Movement, 4*(4), 1.

Meredith, J. E., Fortner, R. W., and Mullins, G. W. (1997). Model of affective learning for nonformal science education facilities. *Journal of Research in Science Teaching, 34*, 805-815, 1997.

Merriam, S. B., & Caffarella, R. S. (1999). *Learning in adulthood.* San Francisco: Jossey-Bass.

National Issues Forum (2009). NIF. Retrieved June 20, 2009, from: http://www.nifi.org/forums/about.aspx

National Park Service. (2009). *National park attendance rises in 2007.* Retrieved March 9, 2009, from http://home.nps.gov/applications/release/Detail.cfm?ID=785.

Norland, E. (2005). The nuances of being "Non": Evaluating nonformal education programs and settings. In E. Norland & C. Somers (Eds.). *Evaluating nonformal education programs and settings,* New Directions in Higher Education, No. 108, (pp. 5-12). San Francisco: Jossey-Bass.

Oldenburg, R. (1989). *The great good place: Cafes, coffee shops, bookstores, bars, salons, and other hangouts at the heart of a community.* Cambridge, MA: DaCapo Press.

Organization for Economic Cooperation and Development. (1973). *Recurrent education: A strategy for lifelong learning.* Paris: Centre for Educational Research and Innovation.

Pedretti, E., Macdonald, R. D., Gitari, W., & McLaughlin, H. (2001). Visitor perspectives on the nature and practice of science: Challenging beliefs through "A Question of Truth." *Canadian Journal of Science, Mathematics and Technology Education, 1*(4), 399-418.

Pratt, D., & Associates. (Eds.). (1998). *Five perspectives on teaching in adult and higher education.* Malabar, FL: Krieger.

Pratt, M. L. (2002). Arts of the contact zone. In J. M. Wolff (Ed.). *Professing in the contact zone* (pp. 1-18). Urbana, IL: NCTE.

Project Wild. (2009). The Council for Environmental Education. Retrieved June 17, 2009, from http://www.projectwild.org/

Reed, H. B. (1984). Nonformal education. In H. B. Reed & E. L. Loughran (Eds.). *Beyond schools: Education for economic, social, and personal development* (pp. 51-72). Amherst, MA: Community Education Resource Center.

Reed, H. B., & Loughran, E. L. (Eds.). (1984). *Beyond schools: Education for economic, social and personal development.* Amherst, MA: Community Education Resource Center.

Rogers, A. (1992). *Adult learning and development.* London: Cassell Educational Limited.

Rogers, A. (2004) *Looking again at non-formal and informal education—towards a new paradigm: The encyclopedia of informal education.* Retrieved April 20, 2009, from www.infed.org/biblio/non_forma l_paradigm.htm

Rogers, A. (2005). *Non-formal education.* Hong Kong: Kluwer Academic Publishers.

San Diego Zoo. (2009). *Sleepover programs at the San Diego Zoo and Wild Animal Park Worldwide Web.* Retrieved April 20, 2009, from http://www.sandiegozoo.org/calendar/sleepovers.html

Silberman-Keller, D. (2006). Images of place and time in non-formal pedagogy. In Z. Bekerman, N.C. Burbules, & D. Silberman-Keller (Eds.). *Learning in places: The informal education reader.* New York: Peter Lang.

Taylor, E. W. (1994). Rethinking adult education for women in Tanzania. *International Education, 23*(1), pp. 30-45.

Taylor, E. W. (2005). Teaching beliefs of nonformal consumer educators: A perspective of teaching in home improvement retail stores in the United States. *International Journal of Consumer Studies, 29*(5), p. 448-457.

Taylor, E. W. (2006). Nonformal education: Practitioner's perspective. *Adult Education Quarterly, 56,* 291-307.

Taylor, E. W., & Caldarelli, M. (2004). Teaching beliefs of nonformal environmental educators: A perspective from state and local parks in the United States. *Environmental Education Research, 10*(4), 451-469.

Taylor, E. W., Parrish, M. M., & Banz, R. N. (2010). Adult education in cultural institutions: Libraries, museums, parks, and zoos. In C. Kasworm, A. Rose, & J. Ross-Gordon (Eds.) *Handbook of adult and continuing education.* Los Angeles: SAGE.

Tilden, F. (2007). *Interpreting our heritage* (4th ed.). Chapel Hill, NC: University of North Carolina Press.

Torres, R. M. (2001, October 7-11). *Amplifying and diversifying learning: Formal, nonformal, and informal education revisited.* Paper prepared for the ADEA Biennial Meeting, Arusha, Tanzania.

The University of Iowa Mobile Clinic. (2009). *An initiative of the University of Iowa health science students.* Retrieved June 15, 2009, from http://www.healthcare.uiowa.edu/Programs/MobileClinic/indexeng.html

Verdurme, A., & Viaene, J. (2003) Consumer beliefs and attitude towards genetically modified food: Basis for segmentation and implications for communication. *Agribusiness, 19*(1), 91-113.

Yakel, E. (2000). Museums, management, media, memory: Lessons from the Enola Gay exhibition. *Libraries & Culture 35*(2), 278-310.

AUTHOR INDEX